T5-AGK-468

SKIING

GOODYEAR PUBLISHING COMPANY, INC.
Pacific Palisades, California 90272

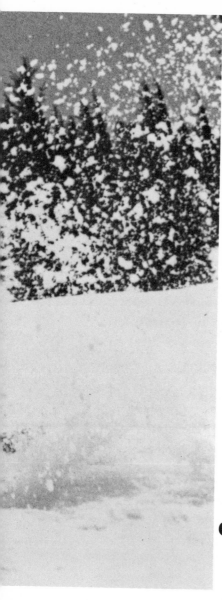

George Twardokens

Art Broten

University of Nevada

SKIING

SKIING

George Twardokens and Art Broten

© Copyright 1971 by
GOODYEAR PUBLISHING COMPANY, INC.
Pacific Palisades, California

All rights reserved. No part of this book may be
reproduced in any form or by any means without
permission in writing from the publisher.

Library of Congress Catalog Card Number: 70-141162

ISBN: 0-87620-849-9   (p)
ISBN: 0-87620-850-2   (c)

Y8499-9   (p)   Y8502-0   (c)

Current printing (last number):
10 9 8 7 6 5 4 3 2 1

Printed in the United States of America

Dedication

We would like to dedicate this book to Ski Patrol members throughout the country. Their devotion to duty, service to safety, and care for skiers is invaluable.

Acknowledgments

Photography: **David Nichols**
Artwork: **Nick Wilson**

Our thanks also to Halina Twardokens for assisting us in the demonstrations.

Contents

SKIING

Introduction and History

INTRODUCTION

This book presents principles which the student can adapt to ever-changing circumstances. The conscientious student will, in addition, investigate current research and special ski articles in order to keep abreast of the latest techniques. The book presents a flexible approach to skiing which allows the student to progress without rigid conformity to a given system. For example, in many instances improved teaching techniques and equipment have opened avenues for a student's rapid progress from basic to advanced maneuvers as well as opening new vistas for more sophisticated skiing. A good skier is recognized as such regardless of the technique he uses.

HISTORY

Man has used various methods of sliding over the snow for over 5000 years. History shows that until more recent times, skis were used mainly for practical purposes such as hunting, military maneuvers, or transportation. At the end of the 19th century, skis were used for little else but walking, running, schussing, and jumping.

As is common in the development of most sports, basic skills and maneuvers are refined until they become rather complicated moves and strategy. Thus

1

in skiing the original practical and survival techniques led to stop turns, stem christies, and linked stem turns starting in the early part of the 20th century.

Norway is credited as being the pioneer for the development of many early ski maneuvers. Christiania, formerly the name of the capitol of Norway, was the origin of the word "christie," commonly used to describe a skidding turn on skis.

Although recreational skiing for university students both in Europe and in America, began as early as 1902, it was enjoyed only by those who could afford to travel to exclusive ski resorts in Switzerland and like areas.

Technically speaking, 1900 to 1935 was the era of stem turns and stem christies, developed by the Austrians with such outstanding instructors as Mathias Zdarsky and Hannes Schneider. This was followed in popularity by the French parallel system, which held the interest of the ski world from 1935 to 1955, and which was led by Emile Allais. There were, of course, many popular variations and modified approaches to these systems.

The years 1955 to 1965 have been known as the "Wedeln Revolution," during which time skiing was again heavily influenced by the Austrians, and more particularly by the well-known Professor Stephan Kruckenhauser.

It may be of interest to note that since 1965 there has been a growing interest in the American Ski Technique.

The ski racing success of a particular country or a particular individual skier, often leads to copying of the techniques by thousands of recreational skiers throughout the world. All too often, however, a particular team style, or the style of an international champion, may be suitable only for his physique, temperament, and background, and not necessarily for other skiers.

Largely on the basis of racing success, diverse skiing systems proliferated at the international level. They became so varied that students, depending upon which school they followed, were taught individual movements as opposed to specific positions. There also arose great differences of opinion on equipment, such as a preference for shorter or longer skis. The result is that in today's ski schools, some stress detailed progressive teaching techniques, while others allow great freedom to the intelligence, ingenuity, and individuality of the instructors.

During the development of skiing, differences in systems became more marked and arguments arose as to which system was superior. The chief antagonists were the French and the Austrians, with an occasional word from the Swiss. Opinions were exchanged, articles were written, and sides were taken; there is even record of a challenge to duel over the proper description of a stem turn.[1]

In 1954, skiing in America became a national collegiate sport. At this time the first National Collegiate Athletic Association ski championships were hosted by the University of Nevada in Reno, Nevada. Since then skiing has become increasingly more widely integrated into the intramural sports programs in colleges and universities throughout the United States. Today, skiing is often found to be a regular offering in the physical education curriculum. In professional preparation European institutions have gone far beyond our own. Teacher training for physical education majors includes 100 to 300 hours of ski instruction as a part of the regular curriculum.

In 1951, various national ski organizations formed "Interski" (International Congress on Ski Instruction) which meets every three years on various continents to demonstrate techniques, exchange ideas, discuss methodology, ski biomechanics, and to present current research papers on the medical aspects of skiing. Interski has also formed a special study group on "school skiing."

A ski instructor who has taught long enough, and has applied himself sufficiently to pass the rigorous *certification examination*, is, today, a well-qualified teacher. France and Austria have highly organized state-supported training centers for ski instructors. Although the United States has yet to establish such state or federally supported training centers, ski instructors may take certification examinations at regional and national ski conventions.

In 1961, certified ski instructors from various regions in the United States formed a national organization called PSIA (Professional Ski Instructors of America). This group represents the United States internationally.

Since 1961, skiing, both as a sport and as a form of recreation, has undergone rapid growth. New lodges and ski resorts have been constructed which, in turn, have opened up to the public new and beautiful winter areas. Modified designs in skis and ski attire have brough a sophistication to the activity which is attracting thousands of new converts each year.

Figure 1.1 shows pins issued by PSIA and by the Far West Ski Instructors Association. These are some of the symbols of proficiency

[1]Professional Ski Instructors of America, "The Official American Ski Technique," The Quality Press, (Salt Lake City: The Quality Press, 1966), p. 140.

for ski instructors. Other geographical divisions use different designs, but similar pins to be worn by certified ski instructors.

Figure 1.1 Instructors Pins for Professional Ski Instructors of America and Far West Ski Instructors Assoc.

Terminology

ABSORPTION Ability to absorb shock over concave and convex terrain by bending and straightening the body joints.

ABSTEMMEN Counter wind-up preceding a turn. Pulling back of uphill shoulder and stemming of downhill ski with following shifts in weight.

AIRPLANE TURN Turning of the skis by the feet in the air after jumping from a mogul.

ANGULATION Moving the body weight laterally by bending the upper body sideways from the waist, and/or turning the knees upslope to control the edges.

ANKLE BEND Bending the lower leg forward so that it forms less than a right angle to the ski.

ANTICIPATION Thinking ahead of maneuvers to be executed, and starting them slightly before the completion of maneuvers being executed.

ARLBERG Refers to St. Anton am Arlberg, Austria—home of Hannes Schneider—father of modern skiing—referred to as the Arlberg Method.

AVALEMENT A shock absorbing effect used to maintain contact with the bumps. Metaphorically speaking, it means to "swallow the bumps."

BACKWARD LEAN   Position of the body when the center of gravity falls behind the balls of the feet.

BANKING   Leaning the body toward the inside of a turn to the point where it counterbalances centrifugal force.

BASE   The bottom running surface of a ski.

BASE SNOW   Old, settled snow which lies beneath freshly fallen snow.

BATHTUB   The indentation made in the snow by a skier falling down. Commonly referred to as a sitzmark.

BINDING   Adjustable attachment which holds the boot to the ski.

BOILER PLATE   Hard-packed, icy snow conditions.

BRAKING   Slowing down of the skis by increasing pressure to the ski edges opposing the direction of travel.

BREAKABLE CRUST   Encrusted snow which is skiable, but may break under the skier's weight.

CAMBER (Bottom)   The arch built into the length of the ski.

CAMBER (Side)   The curve which is cut on both sides of each ski.

CARVING   Using ski turning characteristics such as side cut and flexibility of the skis through purposeful weight shifts and positions to produce a carving track with a minimum of side slipping.

CENTRIFUGAL FORCE   The force which pulls a skier away from the center of his turn.

CENTRIPETAL FORCE   The force (caused by friction on the snow) which attracts the skier toward the center of his turn.

CHECK   A movement, through positioning the body, the skis, or both, used to reduce speed abruptly.

CHOPPED MOGULS   Moguls which have been cut into sharp and dangerous profiles by constant actions of skis. Also a process of completely eliminating moguls with a machine called a mogul chopper.

CHRISTIANIA (CHRISTIE)   Formerly the name of the capitol of Norway. Refers (in skiing) to a turn which is skidded or side slipped.

CLOSED GATE   A gate in a slalom or giant slalom in which the poles are set in line with the racer's path of approach.

COMMA POSITION   Refers to a description of the body position in skidding turns of Austrian Technique.

CORNICE   Wind-drifted snow deposited on the edge of a ridge.

CORN SNOW   A snow condition (usually in the spring) where round crystals are formed by the snow melting in the day, and re-freezing at night. The re-melting of the round crystals on the following day provides "corn" skiing.

CRAMPONNAGE   Retaining the line of a traverse on the uphill edge of the uphill ski, permitting in the meantime, the lower ski to be placed downhill at the desired angle.

CRUD   Heavy, wet snow with a high water content.

DIAGONAL SIDE STEP   Side stepping upward and forward in a walking gait on skis.

DOWNHILL SKI   The ski which is closest to the bottom of the slope.

DOWN UNWEIGHTING   A temporary reduction in the skier's pressure on the snow through a rapid sinking motion.

EDGE CHANGE   In a Traverse, the uphill edges successively become the downhill edges as a result of turning across the fall line.

EDGE CONTROL   Controlling the angle between the bottom of the ski and the surface of the snow by movements of the ankles, knees, and inclination of the body.

EDGING   Placing the weight on the edge of the ski or skis to control sliding.

EDGE SENSE   Ability to feel kinesthetically the position of the edges on the snow.

EDGE SET   Positioning the edges to prevent side slipping. Also positioning the edges as a platform to execute a new movement.

ELBOW GATE   An open and a closed set of gates set at the choice of a course setter for a slalom race.

EXTENSION   Straightening the body as in rising after flexion.

FALL LINE   A fall line is an imaginary line on a slope where a ball would most naturally roll. It is the line of least resistance down a slope from where a skier stands.

FLAT LIGHT   Light conditions on the snow which show no shadows or contrasts, and consequently, hide contours.

FLEXION   Bringing the body members close together.

FLUSH   Three or more closed gates set on, or slightly off the fall line.

FORWARD LEAN   Leaning the body forward so that the center of gravity is in front of the balls of the feet.

FRICTIONAL FORCE   A combination of the snow acting as one resistant surface, and the weight of the bottom of the ski as the other.

GATE   A pair of poles with flags through which a racer must pass as in slalom course.

GIANT SLALOM   A combination of slalom and downhill—A form of alpine racing in which the racer passes through a series of gates which are connected by relatively long traverses.

GRANULAR SNOW   A type of snow which is made up of crystals of frozen snow. It is produced when a frozen crust loses its cohesiveness.

HAIRPIN GATE   A slalom pattern of two closed gates usually set in line with each other.

HARD PACKED   Snow surface which has been machine, ski, or boot packed.

HERRINGBONE   A stepping maneuver used to climb a hill with the skis in a V position and open at the tips.

HOOKING   Most often refers to digging a portion of the skis forcefully into the snow, and producing a curved track around the dug in portion.

HOP CHRISTIE   A parallel turn through the use of unweighting and by retraction of the skis off the snow.

JET TURN   A racing turn discovered by the French which provides a relative acceleration of the body parts and control of the edges.

KICK-TURN   A static turn. From a standing position, one ski is raised clear of the snow and turned in a new direction. This is followed by turning the other around and parallel to it.

LEAD CHANGE   The downhill ski, which is slightly behind in a traverse moves slightly ahead in turning across the fall line, and becomes the leading ski.

LINKING TURNS   Executing a series of turns in alternate directions and in a smooth manner which results in the end of one turn being the beginning of the next turn.

MOGUL   A bump, a series of bumps, or a mound of hard snow that is usually formed by repeated turning actions of many skis in the same place.

MUSCULAR FORCE   Force produced by shortening muscles.

OPEN GATE   A gate used in alpine events, and which is set at right angles to the direction of travel.

OUTRUN   The leveling portion of a slope facilitating reduction of speed or stopping.

PISTE   A European term used to describe a slope packed by skiers or mechanical means.

PLATFORM   A quick displacement and compression of the snow by the skis to provide a flatter surface for a following movement.

POLE BASKETS   Devices near the ends of ski poles which prevent them from penetrating too deeply into the snow.

POWDER SNOW   Dry, light, fluffy snow usually deposited under fairly cold temperatures.

PRE-JUMPING   Jumping, in high speed skiing, before reaching the top of a bump. The pre-jump prevents the skier from being catapulted into the air; consequently shortening the length of the flight and offering greater control.

QUERSPRUNG   A ninety degree jump turn ending in a full stop.

RETRACTION   As the trunk is lifted (up-weighted) the legs are folded slightly under the pelvis. Another form of retraction occurs during the down-unweighting, at which time the tails are lifted upward. This form of movement is known as a "Ruade."

RIVER RUNNING   Refers to skiing in the grooves of a series of moguls.

SCHUSS   Straight downhill run without any braking.

SERPENT TURN   A modern parallel French turn.

SHORT SWING   Consecutive parallel christies without traverse, using a pronounced edge set and a pole plant.

SIDE CUT   (See Figure 4.6) The difference in proportion of the width of a ski between the tip and the tail. (Same as side camber)

SIDE SLIP   Sliding the skis sideways by flattening the edges.

SITZMARK   A depression made in the snow by a skier's fall.

SKATING   Alternate thrusting action of the skis placed at an angle to the forward direction, and duplicating the action of a speed skater.

SLALOM   An alpine race in which the skier runs a course designated by a series of gates set in various combinations. Missing a gate or failure to pass through it properly results in disqualification.

STEMMING   Placing one ski at an angle to the line of descent, and transferring the weight to that ski. If both skis are stemmed simultaneously the term "Plowing" is used.

STOP CHRISTIANIA (STOP CHRISTIE)   A turn in which the skier rapidly arrests momentum when the skis are at a right angle to the fall line.

SWINGING   Descending a slope in linked swing turns.

TAIL   The portion of the ski behind the binding.

TERRAIN JUMP   A technique in which both poles are planted ahead of the skier at the take-off in order to prolong a jump.

TIP   The upward curving portion of the ski in front of the binding.

TRACK   A term used to call out to a person to warn him that he is in line of your descent.

TRACKING   The pattern of grooves in the bottom of a ski plus other design qualities which keep it in a straight line.

TRAVERSE   Skiing across the slope at an angle to the fall line.

TURNING POWER   The energy of force which brings about a rotary change in the direction of the skier.

UNWEIGHTING   A means of reducing the weight on the skis prior to turning so that the skis turn more easily.

UP-UNWEIGHTING   Unweighting by rising (extending) quickly. As the rising motion slows or stops, the skis are unweighted.

WEDELN   A German term which refers to the wagging of a dog's tail. A series of parallel turns made in the fall line.

WEIGHTING   The application of weight to the skis. Usually accomplished by rapid flexion or extension.

Alphabetical Designations

CC   Cross Country

Combi   A ski with a compromise type of construction in order to move well on all types of snow.

DNF   Did not finish

DNS   Did not start

DP   Deep powder

DH   Downhill

DSQ   Disqualified

GS   Giant Slalom

SL   Slalom

ASIA   Alaska Ski Instructors Association

CUSSA   Central United States Ski Association, Certified Instructors Committee

FIS   Federation Internationale de Ski

FWSIA   Far West Ski Instructors Association

ISIA   Intermountain Ski Instructors Association

NASTAR   National Standard Ski Races

NRMSIA   Northern Rocky Mountain Ski Instructors Association

PNSIA   Pacific Northwest Ski Instructors Association

PSIA   Professional Ski Instructors of America

RMSIA   Rocky Mountain Ski Instructors Association

SIA   Ski Industries of America

USEASA   United States Eastern Amateur Ski Association, Certified Professional Ski Teachers Committee

USSA   United States Ski Association

Conditioning

WHY CONDITION

One may undertake a pre-seasonal physical conditioning program, or wait to acquire the conditioning through skiing alone. There are two ways to view the choices:

1. Attempting to condition the body through skiing alone is a rather long process for the average skier. One tires rather easily in the beginning, and it is usually well into the season before the skier is able to spend a full day on the slopes.

2. The skier who engages in a vigorous pre-season conditioning program is usually prepared to ski longer and with more enjoyment. A good pre-season conditioning program requires determination and effort combined with physical discomfort in the beginning stages; however, it does provide the skier with possible additional safety, and greater success as a performer.

In short, omitting the pre-season conditioning program, while not precluding enjoyable skiing, does limit endurance and precludes early progress to higher skill levels.

One should maintain good year-round physical conditioning not only for a specific sport, such as skiing, but also for the purely personal benefit of more effective living. For this reason the authors hereby submit a suggested year-round fitness program.

Spring and Summer. Such activities as swimming, water skiing, hiking, and bicycle riding will all contribute to physical fitness.

Early Fall (General Conditioning Period). Should include running to increase cardio-respiratory efficiency, weight training to strengthen the muscles. Stretching exercises to improve the range of motion may be selected depending upon the need. The American Association for Health, Physical Education and Recreation physical fitness program could be used as a guideline to measure one's level of fitness and progress.[2] It is important from a motivation standpoint to have tables showing national norms for comparison, and to keep written records in order to measure progress. Otherwise, experience has shown that the training period can become sheer, uninspiring drudgery.

Late Fall. These exercises should resemble ski maneuvers. Although there is little specific evidence to show a transfer of *skills* from imitative ski movements performed on dry land to actual ski maneuvers on the snow, *motivation is increased* by changing from general to specific conditioning. It is also important at this stage to strengthen the specific muscle groups involved in actual skiing.

Since, at the present time, there are no specific exercise courses for skiing, one must devise his own. The following suggestions may be helpful. (Note: a stopwatch should be used in exercises 1, 3, 4, and 9 to determine course records for additional motivation):

1. Run a cross-country course with ski poles, using pace variations such as intensive sprints and fast middle distance runs (See Fig. 3.1.)

2. Jump over obstacles using ski poles for support. (See Fig. 3.2.)

3. Jump on both legs through the course with and without the ski poles. (See Fig. 3.3.)

4. Using 10 to 20 old tires, imitate slalom movements by jumping from one leg at a time, and alternating the legs with each jump. (See Fig. 3.4.)

---

[2]*AAHPER Youth Fitness Test Manual,* Revised Edition, (Washington, D.C.: American Association for Health, Physical Education, and Recreation, 1966), pp. 64-5.

Figure 3.1

5. Standing on a block of wood 1″ x 1″ x 1′, Stay in an erect position for one minute without allowing any part of the body to touch the ground. (See Fig. 3.5.)

6. Using the same block of wood, stay in a low position for two minutes without allowing any part of the body to touch the ground. (See Fig. 3.6.)

7. Using the same block of wood, alternate from a low to an erect position 2 to 5 times from the left leg. Repeat this performance from the right leg. Note: Do not bend the leg more than a right angle in executing this exercise. (See Fig. 3.7.)

8. Use a surf roller to imitate slalom maneuvers. (See Fig. 3.8.)

9. Perform a dry land slalom with a series of gates placed close together. Note: The course may be set on hills or on the flat. (See Fig. 3.9.)

10. Strengthen the legs with a *turning board*. There are relatively few muscles which produce an inward rotation of the lower leg. In addition, these muscles are rarely well developed, since this type of movement is infrequent. Conditioning with a

Figure 3.2

Figure 3.3

Figure 3.4

Figure 3.5

turning board will bring about the strength that is so vital to produce a turning motion of the skis. (See Fig. 3.10.)

11. Raise and lower the body. Note: These conditioning movements will aid the skier to "jet" christie maneuvers, and in rising from a fall. (See Fig. 3.11a and b.)

12. Lean against a wall and gradually slide the feet away in order to achieve a stretching movement. (See Fig. 3.12.)

Figure 3.6

Figure 3.7

13. Practice a gradual sagging movement to increase flexibility. (See Fig. 3.13.)

14. Stretch the fingers whenever the hands begin to feel slightly cramped. Note: This is a corrective movement to be used when on the snow. (See Fig. 3.14.)

Figure 3.8

Figure 3.9

Figure 3.10

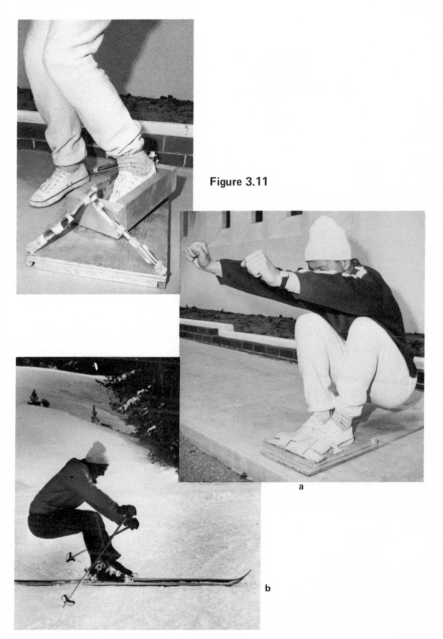

Figure 3.11

a

b

Figure 3.12

Figure 3.13

Figure 3.14

How intensely the individual approaches conditioning depends upon his desire to excel. Should the skier wish to reach his maximum and achieve excellence as a performer, then he will have to exert a great deal of extra effort. If, on the other hand, his goal is simply to enjoy occasional recreational skiing, he will, of course, gear his preparations accordingly.

Locomotion and Downhill Principles

C H A P T E R

LOCOMOTION

Carrying the Skis

Skis may be carried in various ways depending upon how far one wishes to go. Basically, there are 4 accepted methods which combine common sense and common courtesy:

1. For short distances, or in the lodge, carry the skis under the arm. (See Fig. 4.1.)
2. For medium distances, carry the skis on one shoulder, and the poles on the other shoulder as a lever. (See Fig. 4.2.)
3. For hikes and longer distances, carry the skis fastened to a rucksack or pack board. (See Fig. 4.3.)
4. When traveling by bus, train, or plane, place the skis in a ski bag. (See Fig. 4.4.)

Fastening the Skis and Holding the Poles

Although these appear to be simple maneuvers, experience has shown that the following advice is always applicable:

1. Find a level, snow-packed area.
2. Scrape the snow thoroughly from the soles of the boots in order to make the bindings fit properly.

3. Be certain that the safety straps are fastened.
4. Hold the poles in accordance with Figures 4.5 and 4.6.

Figure 4.1

Figure 4.2

Figure 4.3

Figure 4.4

Figure 4.5   **Figure 4.6**

Walking on Skis

Walking on skis resembles normal walking except that the skis are not lifted off the snow. Instead, they are slid, using the poles to aid in propulsion. The right foot and the left pole advance simultaneously as in normal walking.

In the beginning, use a hip-width track on the snow with a ridge in the middle to prevent the tips from crossing. During this stage do not rely too heavily on the pole plant, but rather shift the weight from ski to ski as in a duck waddle. (See Fig. 4.7.)

Climbing on Skis

In climbing parallel to the fall line (See Fig. 4.11), plant the poles in back of the boots as the incline increases. As the incline becomes increasingly steeper, place the skis in a V position and increase the pressure on the inside edge grip (see Fig. 4.8 for an explanation of edge locations) by pressing the knees upslope. This is known as the "herringbone" climb.

Herringbone Climb

From the V position, place all of the weight on one ski as the other ski swings to cut a new step. Repeat the process. Note: Placing the hands on top of the handles of the ski poles, with the poles well in back, will give a more powerful support. (See Fig. 4.9.)

Figure 4.7

Vertical Climbing (Side Stepping)

On steep slopes, place the skis at a right angle to the *fall line*, (See Fig. 4.11), and use the *uphill edges*, (See Fig. 4.8) to cut the steps in the snow. This is accomplished by pressing the knees upslope to make the edges bite. Note: If the skier wishes to traverse as he climbs, he merely, at the initiation of each step, places the uphill ski *forward* as well as *upward*. (See Fig. 4.10.)

DOWNHILL PRINCIPLES

Terrain for Beginning Downhill Runs

Should the skier be able to choose the site, it is best to find a level, snow-packed area on top of the slope in order to get into position for the downhill run. The chosen incline should be gradual, not steep, and should end with a long, level outrun so that the skier may stop without having to brake or turn.

Figure 4.8

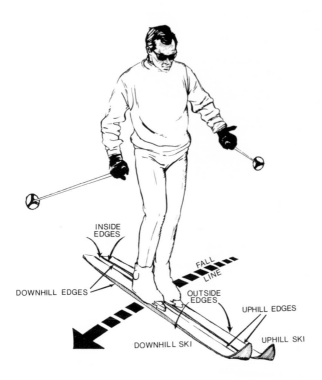

INSIDE
EDGES

FALL
LINE

DOWNHILL EDGES

OUTSIDE
EDGES

UPHILL EDGES

DOWNHILL SKI

UPHILL SKI

If the start is from an incline, the preparations for getting into position for the run are:

1. Stand with the skis across the slope.
2. Twist the trunk of the body toward the downhill side, and plant the poles also on the downhill side approximately 4′ from the downhill ski, and approximately 4′ apart.
3. Place hands on top of the pole handles with the elbows locked, and shift the weight to the poles. (See Fig. 4.12.)
4. Using short steps, move uphill and around until the ski tips are between the poles. (See Fig. 4.13.)
5. Lift the poles to release the weight for the run.

Figure 4.9

Figure 4.10

Figure 4.11

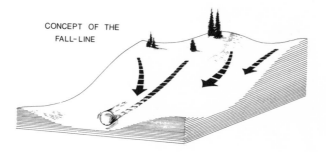

CONCEPT OF THE
FALL-LINE

Figure 4.12

The Downhill Run

There is no specific stance that invariably should be used for a downhill run. Instead, there are several positions which may be used, depending upon the *terrain, snow conditions, and speed.*

Figure 4.13

In his first few downhill runs, the skier will achieve the greatest stability by crouching with the elbows resting upon the thighs, and with the feet placed about hip-width apart. The first few runs may be executed entirely in this fashion. (See Fig. 4.14.)

As the skier gains confidence and becomes more skillful, he assumes more erect positions. This includes a range of movements from the body leaning slightly forward to leaning slightly backward. The feet, however, for the beginner, should still be hip-width apart. The hands should be well apart and ahead of the body with the ski poles pointed backward. The skier should look approximately 20 to 30 yds. ahead. (See Fig. 4.15.)

Varied Terrain and Snow Conditions

As the skier becomes more confident and skillful, the skis may be kept reasonably close together on well-packed snow or deeper snow. However, *if the surface is icy,* the skis should then be separated at approximately hip-width, and pressure should be increased on the inside edges by assuming a "knock-kneed" position. (See Fig. 4.16.)

Figure 4.14

Figure 4.15

Figure 4.16

In skiing from snow of high resistance (unpacked powder) to snow of little resistance (packed), it is necessary to change body positions for changes in speed. For example, in going *from unpacked powder to packed snow* the skier should *lean forward just prior to entering the packed area.* This compensates for the sudden increase in speed on the packed snow.

The opposite, of course, is true when approaching unpacked powder from packed snow. In this case the skier needs to *lean back just prior* to entering the soft snow in order to compensate for the sudden slow-down in speed.

When skiing through a series of dips and swells (usually referred to as large moguls), the skier should attempt *to keep his head at the same level* at all times. In short, *bend the hips, knees, and ankles at the top of the swells,* and *extend the hips, knees, and ankles at the bottom of the dips.* (See Fig. 4.17.)

When the terrain curves upward rapidly, the skier should advance one ski and lean back to compensate so that the momentum does not push him off balance and against the slope. (See Fig. 4.18.)

Figure 4.17

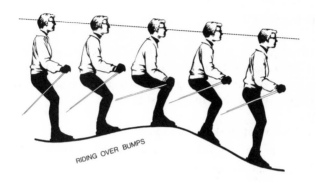

RIDING OVER BUMPS

Figure 4.18

When the slope drops rapidly, the skier should press his knees forward in order to maintain contact with the snow. (See Fig. 4.19.)

Riding the Lifts

The beginning skier usually masters the technicalities of getting on and off the various lifts in three or four rides. These tips are offered to help skiers avoid embarrassing situations and minor irritations when attempting to ride the lifts for the first time.

1. Observe other skiers embarking.
2. If you feel that it is necessary, ask the operator to slow the lift.
3. Select an experienced skier to ride with you.
4. Embark on the same side as the lift operator so that he may be in a position to help you.

Figure 4.19

Approaching Uphill Terrain   Approaching Downhill Terrain

5. Let your partner hold your poles for the first ride.

6. Touch, or grasp lightly, a portion of the chair just prior to sitting down. This aids in anticipating the first contact with the chair.

Tips on Riding T-Bars

1. Set the skis parallel on the track.
2. *Do not sit* on the T-Bar.
3. Keep the legs straight.
4. Grasp the "T" with both hands, elbows slightly bent.

ERRORS AND CORRECTIONS

Walking on Skis

Error. *Lifting* the skis in walking which results in the lack of a glide, and which invites crossing of the skis.

Correction. Prepare a hip-width track in soft snow with a ridge in the center to prevent the skis from crossing. Select terrain which slopes gradually to aid the gliding motion.

Error. Planting the pole *ahead* of the advanced leg which usually results in slipping, or not advancing smoothly.

Correction. Plant the pole, slanting to the back, in the vicinity of the back boot.

Vertical Climbing

Error. *Too little* pressure on the uphill edges which usually results in the skis slipping instead of gripping.

Correction. Press the knees upslope, and exert pressure on the uphill edges.

Error. Taking *too large steps* which usually prohibits pressing the knees upslope and which, in turn, does not allow sufficient pressure to be applied to the uphill edges.

Correction. Take short, "choppy" steps.

Error. Placing the skis at other than a right angle to the fall line which usually results in slippage and awkwardness.

Correction. Place the skis precisely at a right angle to the fall line, and plant the poles in line with the boots.

Downhill Running

Error. Taking the *first* downhill run without warming up or becoming acquainted with the equipment and snow conditions.

Correction. Before taking the first downhill run, select a slope with a slight grade, and practice walking movements, short glides, side stepping, and small hops in place.

Error. Fear of increased speed usually brings about an *exaggerated straightening* and *stiffening* of the ankles, and *also an exaggerated bending of the knees*. This usually results in a backward position with the center of gravity too far behind the boots. In short, the skier, by assuming this position, inadvertently aids the skis to slip out from under him. (See Fig. 4.20.)

Correction. Bend the *knees less,* and the *ankles more* to the extent that the shins press against the tops of the boots. This will keep the upper body in a vertical line over the ski bindings, thus retaining the center of gravity in proper line.

Figure 4.20

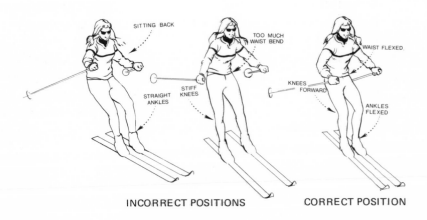

INCORRECT POSITIONS   CORRECT POSITION

Error. An exaggerated forward lean, with the poles held in front of the legs, usually invites a forward fall. (See Fig. 4.20.)

Correction. Bend the knees, straighten the hip joints, and hold the poles in front of the hips (wider apart if lateral balance is unsteady) with the pole baskets well behind the body.

Beginning Turns

THE SNOWPLOW

The snowplow position is assumed by placing the skis in a V position with the tips approximately 6″ apart. The weight should be placed evenly on both skis with pressure exerted on the inside edges. (See Fig. 5.1.)

In assuming this position for the first time, the skier should start on level terrain with the skis held together while the poles are planted for support approximately 4′ apart and directly in front of the tips. The skier may then place one leg at a time in the snowplow position, or, if preferred, hop to the position. By placing the poles in back and pushing himself forward for a short distance, the skier will obtain a "feeling" of the inside edges sliding over the snow. This also allows the skier to realize that the snowplow glide entails a coordinated movement of the *hips, knees,* and *ankles.* For example, the hip joints control the *opening* and *closing* of the skis, while the knees and ankles control the gliding adjustment on the inside edges. More specifically, as the knees are bent forward and pressed inward, the amount of inside edging is increased.

As the beginner progresses from level terrain to a gradual downhill slope, additional confidence and

Figure 5.1

control may be acquired by alternately widening and narrowing the track during a slow glide.

To stop from a *slow* snowplow glide, merely widen the V position and press downward over the heels. Note: The snowplow should not be used for braking at high speeds, for the beginner may cross his skis, with a resultant injury. If in an uncontrolled speed situation and a fall appears unavoidable, lower the body and fall backward and to the right or left side. If a fall appears unavoidable on a traverse, lower the body and fall toward the uphill side. As a matter of safety and courtesy for other skiers, one should always fill the resulting "sitzmark" before going on.

To arise from a fall on the slope, place the skis together on the downhill side and across the fall line. Next, *place the heels in back of, or in line with, the hips,* press the hand on the snow, and come to a standing position. If the snow is soft, use the poles as indicated in Figure 5.2.

THE SNOWPLOW TURN

A simple weight shift against one of the skis will initiate a turning movement in a snowplow glide close to the fall line. Shifting the weight to

Figure 5.2

the left ski will start a turning movement to the right; likewise, a weight shift to the right ski will start a turning movement to the left. The turn becomes a bit more involved if executed while moving across a slope. In this case, a twisting of both knees in the direction of the turn with *increased* pressure on the *uphill* ski edge, and *decreased* pressure on the *downhill* ski edge, coupled with momentum, will complete the turn. (See Figure 5.3) Note: Various ski systems advocate different methods as a part of the turning force. Some stress heel pressure; others stress weight transfer; still others stress steering the whole body in the direction of the turn. The authors believe that a good ski instructor teaches that method which is in line with natural laws as they apply to bodies in motion, and more particular, to the body type and personality of the learner.

One may use snowplow turns to join traverses; however, the V position is only a transitory learning stage, and not an end in itself. The skier should progress as quickly as possible to more graceful and skillful turns.

Figure 5.3

THE TRAVERSE

In the traverse the skis are held to the snow by the uphill edges. The *uphill ski* is kept *slightly forward,* as well as the boot, knee, and hip joint. The knees are pressed forward and upslope while the *upper body* compensates by leaning downslope, and over the downhill ski. More weight is placed on the downhill ski. In the beginning, for increased stability, the skis may be held as much as 1′ apart. Later, to develop more elegance, the skis should be held closer together if snow conditions permit. (See Figs. 5.4 and 5.5.)

The bite, or pressure, on the edges, must be increased as the slope becomes steeper or harder. This is accomplished by pressing the knees upslope, and is made easier on hard snow by having sharp edges on the skis, and boots with good ankle support.

To execute a true traverse, the object is to keep the center of gravity on the edges at the center of the skis. Any significant deviation toward the sides or fore and aft makes the edging less efficient, and may result in curving or slipping. For example, if the edging is too light, and the weight is pressed too far forward, the ski tips will tend to slip down. Conversely, if the edging is too light and the weight is shifted to the back of the skis, the tails will tend to slip down. If the edge pressure is stronger, and the weight is shifted too far forward, the skis will tend to curve uphill.

When moving skis are edged and weighted, the *tips* will tend to cut more into the snow than other portions of the skis. This cutting action promotes a turning of the skis in the direction of the tips. The approximate proportion of ski tip to waist to tail (as viewed from the top) is 9:7:8 (See Fig. 5.6).

THE STEM TURN

Here the V position is held only during the turning phase. The skier starts and ends the maneuver in a traverse position. At slower speeds one may link traverses with snowplow turns. However, as the speed increases, one may be taught to stem with only the upper ski. (See Fig. 5.7.)

Stemming is started by shifting the bodyweight to the downhill ski, lifting the uphill ski tail and placing it upslope in order to turn the ski onto its inside edge, and all the while keeping the ski tips even. As the *turning* and *braking* begin, the weight is shifted gradually against the uphill (now called the outside) ski. The progressive weighting on the outside ski will bring it around in an arc so that it progressively becomes the lower weighted ski. *Until the skis meet the fall line the edging should be the same as in a snowplow turn*, i.e., pressing both knees in the direction of the turn. *After passing the fall line*, the inside ski must be turned partially and start to lead the maneuver. A *skidding sensation* of the skis near the end of the turn is a welcome sign of progress. Note: Some schools

Figure 5.4

Figure 5.5

Figure 5.6

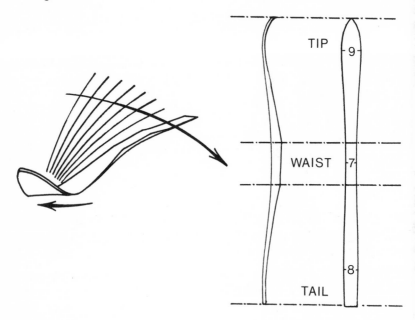

advocate an active turning of the inside ski so that the uphill edge *brushes* the snow downward, and helps to pull the skis together in the final maneuver.

Points to Remember

The stem turn is brought about by:

1. Weight change
2. Ski carving ability.
3. Proper edging.
4. Momentum.

The stem turn also has the following elements of more advanced turns:

1. Edge change. (See Fig. 5.8.)
2. Weight change.

3. Lead change.
4. Partial turning of the inside ski.

In addition, the stem turn provides a foundation for stem christies, besides being a practical turn for heavy and difficult snows.

Figure 5.7

Figure 5.8

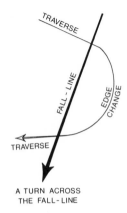

A TURN ACROSS
THE FALL-LINE

ERRORS AND CORRECTIONS

The Snowplow

Error. Uneven edging of the skis. The ski which is edged stronger will force the direction of the descent.

Correction. From a stationary V position on the flat, practice an *even* raising and lowering of the outside edges at various angles by narrowing and widening the gap between the knees and incorporating the ankles.

Error. Uneven weight distribution on the skis which results in losing the V position.

Correction. Practice hopping from snowplow position to a parallel position. Try to land simultaneously with both skis.

Error. An exaggerated forward lean from the waist which causes a tightening of the back muscles, and may easily bring about a crossing of the skis.

Correction. Hold the pelvis on a balanced vertical line with the trunk. Carry the body on an erect skeleton, rather than on tense back muscles.

Snowplow Turns

Error. Opposing the turn by keeping the *inside edge* of the lower ski edged too strongly. (Unreleased.)

Correction. Flatten the edge of the downhill ski by pushing the lower knee downslope.

Error. Placing the bodyweight over the outside ski at the turn *instead of against the ski,* which often results in "catching" an outside edge.

Correction. Keep the hips *between* the skis. Shift the weight *against,* not over, a well-positioned edge toward the outside of the turn.

Error. Keeping the tips too widely separated, which causes the skis to rest sharply on the *inside* edges, and prevents turning.

Correction. Keep the tips about 6″ apart. Steer actively with the outside leg of the turn.

The Traverse

Error. Holding the skis evenly abreast, thus inviting a cramped position and a possible crossing of the skis.

Correction. Hold the *uphill* ski slightly in advance. Tilt the uphill pelvis socket forward.

Error. Holding the downhill hip socket ahead of the uphill hip socket, thus bringing about an unnatural and cramped position.

Correction. Practice a stationary correct traverse position. This may seem unnatural at first, but will become better understood and "sensed" after a practice session.

The Stem Turn

Error. Placing the tip of the uphill ski ahead of the downhill ski while stemming, which results in an improper weight transfer and a possible crossing of the skis.

Correction. While stemming, retract the uphill ski so that its tip is placed several inches behind the tip of the downhill ski.

Error. Performing the turn within too small a radius, which makes it difficult to turn the inside ski.

Correction. Select a shallower slope, and perform the maneuver within a larger radius.

Intermediate Turns

As beginning turns are mastered, the foundation is set for intermediate turns. These are usually more interesting because of the increased challenge to skills, and the ultimately more graceful movements.

Thus far in the text, the skier has been presented with steered (platform) turns where the skis, during the turning phase, have been in a V position. The intermediate turns across the fall line are *partially steered and partially skidded*. The *skidding* or *side slipping* element is an integral part of all "christie" type turns.

PREREQUISITES

The prerequisites for skidding turns are as follows:

1. Unweighting.
2. Side slipping.
3. Turning force.
4. Re-edging.
5. Weighting.

Unweighting

This is a momentary reduction or elimination of the skier's weight on the skis, and therefore on the snow.

It is an aid in initiating and executing turns since light skis and a reduction of friction on the snow permit easier changes of direction.

There are various ways in which one may unweight. Some of the most-often-used methods are:

1. *Up-unweighting.* Achieved by thrusting the body upward with a forceful surge, and a quick straightening of the legs. The skier prepares by assuming a crouching position. (See Fig. 6.1.)

2. *Down-unweighting.* Achieved by dropping quickly to a crouching position. In preparation for this type of unweighting, the skier first starts from a fairly erect position. (See Fig. 6.1.)

3. *Stepping from ski to ski.*

There are additional forms of unweighting. These will be discussed in a later section.

Figure 6.1

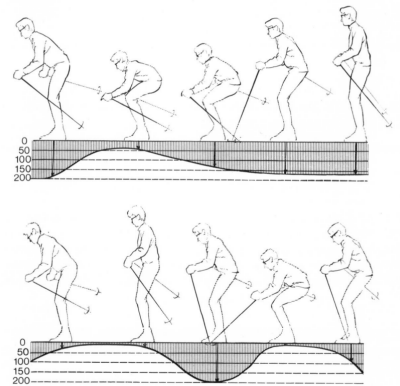

Side Slipping (Skidding)

This is performed with the skis parallel and resting on the uphill edges. A major portion of the weight rests on the downhill ski. Side slipping is used both for "braking" and for losing altitude. Side-slipping also helps to develop a very important aspect of skiing which may be termed the "kinesthetic sense." This is a muscular sense of the edge positions in relation to the snow. "Edge sense" is essential for more advanced ski maneuvers.

There are numerous methods for starting a slide slipping movement from a traverse, all of which have the common purpose of diminishing or releasing the grip of the ski edges on the snow. The usual methods include laterally bending the ankles, pressing the knees toward the downhill side, or combinations of both.

The feeling of skidding the edges over the snow has already been experienced in the snowplow, or possibly in traversing a slope with incorrect weight placement. However, side slipping vertically (broadside) for several feet with the skis held close together is a difficult maneuver.

Before attempting a classic side slip, the skier should practice the following:

1. *Starting a slipping movement from a snowplow.* Start from the fall line in a snowplow position. Next, release one edge (right or left) and place more weight on the ski with the released edge. Slide downhill for several feet. To stop the sliding motion, re-edge the released ski by pressing the knee inward, and return to a straight snowplow glide with the weight and edges evenly distributed. Repeat this maneuver in the opposite direction. (See Fig. 6.2.)

2. *Miniature Slips.* Stand in traverse position supported by the poles which are placed on the fall line. "Play" with the edges by pressing the knees toward the slope so that the edges "bite." Next, flatten the edges as much as is necessary to slip downhill two or three inches. Stop by pressing the knees upslope. Repeat this exercise 20 to 30 times. (See Figs. 6.3 and 6.4.)

Note: Avoid pushing the knees too far toward the downhill side since there is the hazard of catching a downhill edge and falling. Be gentle with the knee action during the maneuver, and release the edges gradually. It is better, in the beginning, to release with too little action rather than too much.

Figure 6.2

Figure 6.3

Figure 6.4

Vertical Side Slip

Terrain.   Choose an area with a steep but short and well-packed mogul or incline. Start from a traverse position.

Position.   Hold the skis parallel and ready to drop down the fall line broadside.

Starting.   Relax the ankles and leg muscles, and "roll" both skis with an even motion toward the downhill side. (See Figs. 6.5 and 6.6.)

If slipping does not occur immediately, aid the movement by pressing the knees gently toward the downhill side. You may further aid this movement by pushing against the slope with the uphill pole, or both poles. (See Figs. 6.7 and 6.8.)

As the slide begins, "freeze" the position and ride with control as far as possible. Note: Control of position over the skis must be maintained. Balancing movements of the hands and body easily influence the direction of the side slip.

Figure 6.5

Figure 6.6

Figure 6.7

Figure 6.8

One may also start a side slip with a single rising movement. This is done by relaxing the ankles and straightening the knees which cancels the angulated position at the traverse, and starts the slide.

Another method of starting a side slip is to crouch rapidly. This movement overpowers the edge grip by a momentary reduction of weight on the edge grip, and brings the knees in line with the skis. Either method is acceptable; the main point is to make the skis slip broadside.

Direction of the Side Slips. Side slips may proceed in various directions, and will form different patterns in the snow. On a smooth terrain the principles of weight placement, and the *amount* of edging dictates the direction of the slip.

Example #1. When the edging is gentle, placing the weight toward the tips will cause them to drop. Likewise, placing the weight toward the back of the skis will cause the tails to drop.

Example #2. When the edging is stronger, placing the weight toward the tips will cause them to curve (hook) and the tails to slide. Placing the weight toward the tails will cause them to hook while the tips seek the fall line. (See Fig. 6.9.)

Note: The action in Example #2 usually occurs after a slight delay, and causes a more curving side slip uphill or downhill.

Perhaps the most-often-practiced maneuver is side slipping diagonally to the fall line (forward and downward). This movement is started by skiing in a traverse where, after an edge release, the momentum keeps the side slip in motion. A good practice routine is to start the diagonal side slip, re-edge to return to the traverse, and then release the edges for another diagonal side slip. Repeat this process in a series of moves.

Side slipping the tails and hopping back to an original traverse is a more advanced variation of this exercise.

Figure 6.9 Directions of side slips.

Example 1   Example 2

Turning Force

This might be described as a turning of the whole body, or parts of the body, immediately in the direction of the turn, which initiates the change in the direction of the skis. Depending upon the degree of the turn, a portion of the body will tend to move in the direction of the turn. This may be divided into body parts mainly active in affecting the radius of the turn. The division is as follows (See Fig. 6.10.):

1. Turning the feet.
2. Pressing the knees toward the inside of the turn.
3. Moving the legs in the hip socket in the direction of the turn.
4. Moving the legs and the hips in the direction of the turn.
5. Moving the entire body in the direction of the turn.

Figure 6.10

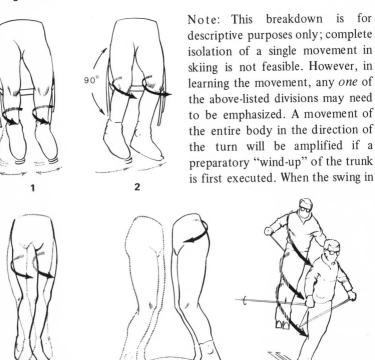

Note: This breakdown is for descriptive purposes only; complete isolation of a single movement in skiing is not feasible. However, in learning the movement, any *one* of the above-listed divisions may need to be emphasized. A movement of the entire body in the direction of the turn will be amplified if a preparatory "wind-up" of the trunk is first executed. When the swing in the direction of the turn is under way, the muscles of the body must be tightened to convey the turning force to the skis.

A movement of the legs alone in the direction of the turn needs resistance from the trunk, which should remain stable. This permits the legs to turn against a stable mass. When skis are unweighted, the turning force quickly changes the direction of the skis.

In review, there are many forces which affect the radius of a turn. Basically, these forces are:

1. Muscular force.
2. Gravitational force.
3. Ski construction.

Muscular force keeps the skier in a balanced position, and precipitates turning. Proper edging and weighting of the skis, coupled with gravitational pull, help the skis move in a smooth arc. Deflecting force, or snow resistance, is needed for controlled turnings as opposed to gyrating freely around the body mass.

Re-Edging

Skis are held *flat* on the snow, as in walking on level terrain and in skiing a downhill run in a fall line, or they are held on the *edges,* as in climbing, traversing, and turning.

The *degree of edging* depends upon snow conditions, speed, and the radius of the turn.

An increase or decrease of edging actions is the final result of moving body parts from side to side. The skier may achieve various degrees of quickness and strength of edging depending upon which body parts and joints are called upon to exert effort. Some examples are as follows:

Edging with Lateral Movements of the Ankles and Feet. This action is *fast,* but *weak* and *limited in range* due to the poor leverage of the muscles, and the relative confinement of the modern ski boot.

Edging Turning the Thighs and Knees to the Side. This action is *fast* and *strong,* and *covers a wide range.*

Edging by Moving the Pelvis from Side to Side. This action is *powerful* but *slow,* and *covers a wide range.*

Edging by Tilting the Whole Body Sideways (Banking). This action is *powerful* but *slow,* and requires good support of the edges on the snow. It *covers a wide range.* (See Fig. 6.11.)

Figure 6.11

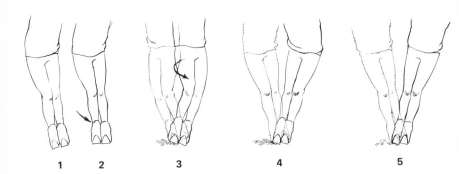

Skidding occurs when forces act upon the edges which, in turn, press upon the snow with enough power to displace it. An angle between the ski and the snow which "banks up" snow under the ski is needed to prevent skidding. In short, edging is a composite movement of body parts and joints depending upon how quick and how strong the skier desires the re-edging to be. The most common form of re-edging is performed by a synchronized movement of the thighs, ankles, and feet.

Weighting

This is a momentary *increase* of the skier's wieght upon the skis (and snow) through manipulation of body weight. It is intended to produce firm contact with the snow, and thus helps the skis carve a turn, and increases stability. Note: At this point the reader may be confused as to exactly when weighting and unweighting occur, since they are both achieved by *quickly* raising or lowering the body. For the sake of clarification, examples as follows are submitted:

1. **Straightening the body quickly from a crouch.** In this instance the weight is increased at first, and then is reduced toward the top of the upward movement.

2. **Dropping the body quickly into a crouch.** In this instance the weight is reduced at first, and then increased. Note: Weighting and unweighting cannot be acquired successfully through a slow or gradual movement.

3. **Stepping from ski to ski.** Here, the skier's weight on the snow does not change, but is simply shifted from one ski while the other becomes unweighted and is free to maneuver, as in starting a stem turn, or in climbing.

CHRISTIE INTO THE HILL

This is a skidding parallel turn which starts from a fall line or a traverse. It is executed on the same set of edges without a change of the leading ski. In short, it is a dynamic synthesis of the following unfolding moves:

1. Unweighting.
2. Side slipping.
3. Turning force.
4. Edging.
5. Weighting.

There are two standard approaches in the execution of this maneuver. Both are quite acceptable, and the skier may choose the one best suited to the situation. These approaches are as follows:

Approach #1. Start a traverse from a fairly erect position and gather momentum. Next, sink rapidly in order to unweight the skis and to relax the grip of the edges. Start a side slip, and direct it by pivoting the legs so that the ski tips carve uphill, and the tails slide downhill. Continue this movement briefly. Start re-edging by tensing the ankles and placing the knees and hips toward the inside of the turn, while compensating with the upper body toward the outside of the turn. The more nearly the skier approaches a right angle to the fall line, the more weight is placed on the downhill ski. (See Fig. 6.12.)

Approach #2. Start from a traverse, then lower to a crouched position. Spring up and forward to unweight the skis and relax the edge grip. Again, side slip and direct the skid so that the tips move uphill, and the tails slide downhill. Lower the body for re-edging and weighting. (See Fig. 6.13.)

The maneuver may be brought to a halt by increasing the edging and bringing the skis more across the fall line, or by stepping uphill until the momentum is lost. Note: It is possible at high speeds to perform a christie

Figure 6.12

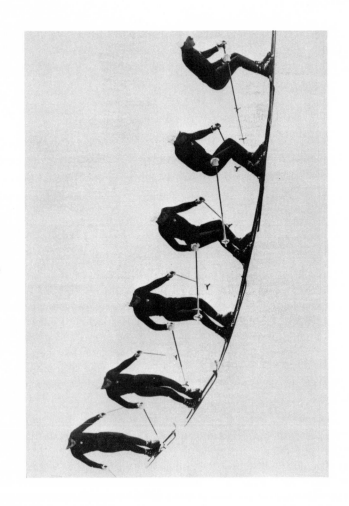

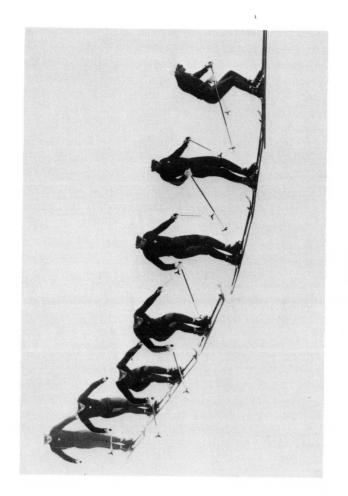

Figure 6.13

into the hill where many of the listed elements, such as unweighting, become unperceivable. At high speeds a christie into the hill, as a second part of a christie across the fall line, has in evidence only steering and edging.

STEM CHRISTIE

A stem christie permits the skier to cross the fall line through a partially steered and partially skidded turn.

The *longer* and *wider* the V position is held, the more elementary the maneuver becomes, thus permitting a safe turn only at slower speeds. On the other hand, the *narrower* and *shorter* the V position is held, the more advanced the turn becomes and permits the maneuver to be executed at higher speeds.

A stem christie prepares a new edge and direction of descent against which the weight is shifted to serve as a major turning force. The initial unweighting which facilitates the change of edges is performed by stepping from ski to ski. The V position, at the moment of the initiation of the turn, gives the skier a more stable position. One may start a stem christie by stemming the uphill ski, the downhill ski, or both skis at once.

Stemming the Uphill Ski. This directs the ski more in the desired direction of descent.

Stemming the Downhill Ski. This may serve as a check of speed.

Stemming Both Skis. This permits the skier to steer as long as desired before skidding the skis.

The initiation of the skidding phase of the turn may start from a crouched V position followed by a rising movement to close the skis. It may also start from an erect position followed by a sinking movement to draw the skis together. Stemming a downhill ski, and stemming of both skis, are performed with a sinking motion. Stemming an uphill ski can be executed from either an erect or a low position. Higher speeds than normally used for a christie into the hill, and convexed forms of terrain, will facilitate the turning and skidding of the edges.

Variations of a Stem Christie

Stem Christie From a High Position. (See Fig. 6.14.) After selecting a favorable terrain for the initiation of the maneuver, the skier gathers momentum in a traverse. While traversing in an erect position, most of the

Figure 6.14

weight is transferred to the downhill ski to permit the uphill ski to be
retracted, stemmed, and placed on the inside edge. The skier now pushes
his weight off the well-edged downhill ski against the uphill ski, turns the
leg in the direction of the turn, and sinks. When the outside ski responds
to this steering action by skidding, the downhill ski is drawn parallel,
slightly ahead, and on the outside edge. As the feet and skis are displaced

to the side by skidding, the knees and hips are pressed toward the center of the turn, and the upper body compensates by leaning outward. Note: This body position resembles a "comma," and this term is often used in skiing literature. The maneuver continues as a christie into the hill as described in Approach #1 and Figure 6.12.

Stem Christie From a Low Position. (See Fig. 6.15.) Terrain and speed should be similar to a christie from a high position. The new edge is

Figure 6.15

prepared on the uphill ski while lowering the body position by bending the legs and hip joints. While rising, the weight is transferred against the stemmed ski, and the legs are straightened to project the body upward and forward. The inside ski is brought parallel and advanced slightly on its outside edge. The turn continues as a christie into the hill. (Again, refer to Approach #1).

STEM CHRISTIE FROM A LOW POSITION AND ROTATION

This is a christie with a stem and turning motion of the body in the direction of the turn while straightening.

General Remarks:

An uphill or downhill ski may be stemmed for an initiation of a turn.

The turning force comes from a projection of the whole body in the direction of the turn.

Banking the body toward the inside of the turn makes the edge hold to the snow.

When the uphill stem is used, the ski may be placed flat on the snow or slightly on the edge.

The pole may be used for additional support at the initiation of the turn.

Preparation. Terrain and speed are the same as in previous stem christies:

1. Place the uphill ski in a stem position flat or slightly on the edge.
2. Position the tip of the downhill pole—ready to plant it.
3. Bend the body joints, especially the downhill leg, but keep the downhill ski well-edged and weighted.

Initiation and Steering

1. Start straightening the body and plant the inside pole to use it as additional support and a pivoting point.[3]

---

[3]*Pole Plant:* Halfway between the ski tip and boot and 2′ to the side are the standard placement for this type of a turn. Principles of pole planting are discussed in Chapter 7.

2. With a straightening movement, shift the weight against the outer ski, and project the body up forward and around in the direction of the turn.

3. Lift the heel of the downhill ski and change its edge.

4. Control the radius of the turn by steering the entire body and banking (forward and around to the inside of the turn).

Stemming With the Downhill Ski: To obtain the V position from a traverse, one may push the downhill ski to a stem by releasing the downhill edge, as in side slipping, or by exerting additional weight on it so that it is forced to drop without much change in the edge angle. If snow conditions and the angle between the edge and the snow are such that the ski compresses a bank of snow under its surface, the downhill stem will serve not only as a check of speed, but also will build the snow into a platform. From this platform, the skier may gain firm support while straightening the lower leg, thus obtaining a rebound from it with greater comfort and efficiency.

Numerous combinations for performing a stem christie are used by various ski schools. Some teach a total parallel system, and do not use a stem christie at all.

General Characteristics of Stem Christies

1. The unweighting is performed in two stages:
   a. The outside ski is completely unweighted.
   b. The weight is shifted to the outside ski.
2. The edges change position in succession: outside ski edge first, followed by the inside ski edge.
3. Most of the skidding is obtained by shifting the weight from the downhill ski to the uphill ski.
4. The V position gives the skier better balance at the critical moment of starting the skid, and changing the edges.

ERRORS AND CORRECTIONS

Introduction

Up to this point elementary maneuvers could be learned at slow or moderate speeds. The more intricate maneuvers, however, introduce the subtler aspects of turning forces, weighting, and unweighting, and require faster speeds and more edging precision. Errors will surface more quickly now due to such things as faulty equipment (e.g., skis which are too long), physiological drawbacks (e.g., lack of muscular strength or acclimatization), or psychological aspects (e.g., fear of increased speeds). A good ski instructor will advise the skier on a need for proper or better ski equipment. Overcoming physiological or psychological obstacles may, however, take longer to achieve.

Christie Into the Hill

Error. Lack of a skidding motion due to an inability to release the edges.

Correction. Return to the practice of all forms of side slipping with particular reference to a diagonal side slip.

Error. Leading the turn with the *lower* hip socket resulting in "over" turning and crossing the tips.

Correction. Practice traverses and displacement of the ski tails downhill while holding the correct angulated position.

Stem Christie

Error. Inability to enter the skidding phase of the turn due to edging the *outside* ski of the turn too strongly.

Correction. At the moment of stemming, place the stemmed ski almost flat on the snow before transferring weight against it.

Error. Selecting too small a radius for the turn, resulting in an inability to perform the maneuver smoothly which requires brushing the inside ski next to the outside ski.

Correction. Since a larger turning radius develops more speed, the skier must first overcome the psychological fear of increased speeds by practicing downhill runs on terrains which terminate in an upward rise so that the speed is slowed naturally.

Parallel Turns

PARALLEL CHRISTIE

A parallel christie connects two opposite traverses, and is executed, from beginning to end, with skis parallel and close together. The edges of both skis should be changed simultaneously by rolling them toward the inside of the turn. (See Figure 7.1 which illustrates a parallel turn with counter rotation as a turning force.)

The above description denotes a *classic* parallel christie or "pure christie" in a traditional sense. There are other advanced turns which do not necessarily comply with this description.

The difficulty in executing a parallel christie lies in providing a turning impulse which will turn the tips and tails of both skis at once and, at the same time, change both edges.[4] To overcome the difficulty of the turn in the early stages of learning, the skier may incorporate pronounced unweighting coupled with the choice of convexed forms of terrain to aid the turning and changing of edges. The use of ski poles for support and timing helps to trigger the turn in

---

[4] The difficulty in displacing the tips and tails of the skis lies in the first 90° of the turn. The ideal turn should follow the symmetry of a half circle.

Figure 7.1

place of sheer muscular effort which, at this stage, is commonly weak and uncoordinated. Later, as the skier becomes better conditioned, and the christie becomes more refined, muscular turning force becomes a more dominant aspect in triggering the turn.

Characteristic Phases of a Parallel Turn

1. Preparation (Getting Set).
2. Release or Initiation (Triggering the Turn).

3. Steering Phase (Middle Phase or Guiding Phase).
4. Finishing (New Traverse or Stopping).

Descriptions of the four characteristic phases of a parallel turn are as follows:

Preparation. This might be termed "getting set" for starting the turn. For example, it is like compressing a steel spring to prepare it for rapid expansion, or like stretching a rubber band to prepare it for rapid contraction. Classic forms of preparation entail (1) assuming a low position in preparation for a quick energetic rise of the body, or (2) assuming an erect position in preparation for a rapid flexion of the body. Note: Anticipating the turn by leaning the body toward the downhill side is, as of this date, a more recently developed form of preparation. (This is discussed in more detail in Chapter 8.)

Release. This is the most difficult aspect of the turn, for several movements must be performed almost simultaneously. The movements should result in a series of actions as follows:

1. Unweighting.
2. Turning impulse.
3. Leverage.
4. Edge change.
5. Lead change.
6. Weight distribution.
   a. *Unweighting.* Any form of unweighting may be used, short of stepping from ski to ski. The important effect should be the reduction of pressure (grip) of the edges in the traverse.
   b. *Turning Impulse.* This is the muscular force which changes the direction of the skis by displacing them downhill. This is a circular motion of the body and may originate from many sources as described in Chapter 6 and shown in Figure 6.10. In connection with the turning force (impulse), ski instructors commonly use two terms: *rotation* and *counter rotation*. Rotation is a motion around the vertical axis of the body in the direction of the turn. *Counter rotation* is a quick turning motion in one part of the body resulting in a counter action in another part of the body when resistance is markedly reduced. In addition to these terms, there is an action called *split rotation* which is an application of rotation and counter

rotation for turning. Any one method may serve for initiating a turn with the remainder of the effort used for steering. More specifically, the turn may be started by rotating the body, followed by counter rotation during the remaining phase.

c. *Leverage.* This is the result of a forward or backward lean of the body (fore and aft), i.e., toward the tips or the tails of the skis. A forward lean is achieved when the skier places his center of gravity ahead of the balls of his feet. A backward lean is achieved when the skier places his center of gravity in back of the balls of his feet. In a standard parallel turn a slightly forward lean is most often used. Leaning forward helps to maintain balance (fore and aft) and compensates for increases in speed as the skier approaches the fall line. A backward lean requires more strength and athletic ability, and is more evident in advanced and sophisticated turns.

d. *Edge Change.* Edge changes are a *must* for downhill turns which cross the fall line. As a reminder, edge changes are described in detail in Chapter 6 (Figure 6.11)

e. *Lead Change.* During the release, the downhill ski of the traverse should be pushed gradually forward approximately one half of a boot length. This ski will then become the inside advanced or leading ski of the turn. Although lead change is not an absolute must in a downhill turn, it does help to prevent the tips from crossing, and puts the skier's legs in a more comfortable position while turning.

f. *Weight Distribution.* Before starting the turn, more weight should be on the downhill ski. During the initiation the weight should be shifted toward the outside ski of the turn. Some techniques stress equal weight distribution to both skis at the preparation and initiation of the turn.

Steering Phase. As the skis begin to skid during the turning phase, the skier should direct the skid by regulating the amount of edging and muscular turning force. A *lesser amount of edge pressure* will result in a *greater amount of skidding* and a wider track on the snow, while a *greater amount of edge pressure* will cause a narrower track and a *lesser amount of skidding*. This is partially caused by the carving characteristics of the skis. Depending upon the technique used, either *banking*, or an *angulated position* achieves the effect.

Finishing. To come to a stop, the skier should increase the amount of edging, and steer the skis across the fall line until the momentum stops. To link the turns, the skier should select a desired angle for the traverse before eliminating the skid by re-edging.

THE POLE PLANT AND TERRAIN

The pole plant may be used in the early stages of the stem christie, particularly when snow conditions create greater resistance to turning. During parallel turns, however, the pole is planted, most of the time, at the initiation of the turn. Plant the right pole for a right turn, and the left pole for a left turn.

The pole serves as a support in helping balancing movements of the body at the difficult moment in initiating christies. As the skier pushes on the pole he receives an additional upward lift which facilitates the unweighting. The pole plant also serves as a timing device, for it gives the signal for the initiation. In addition, it may also serve as a pivoting point, and as an aid to start the displacement of the skis. Maximum use of the pole occurs when the weight is placed upon it, not where it first makes contact with the snow.

As a general rule, *for long, sweeping turns the pole should contact the snow near the tips of the skis* where it serves more as a timing device. *For shorter turns the pole serves more for support, and should be planted in line with the boots toward the downhill side of the slope.* [5]

For highly advanced turns beyond the parallel turn, the pole is planted in back of the boots where it serves strongly as a pivoting point, and also as a push-off point to increase acceleration.

In the early learning stages, as in walking and climbing on skis, propulsion is obtained by pushing on the planted pole or poles. (For correct position of pole placement on various radii of the turns, see Figures 7.1, 7.3, 7.5, 8.1, and 8.2.)

Terrain, snow conditions, and speed may, in some manner, help or hinder turning on skis.

If the skier is on a mogul, i.e., on convex terrain, only the bottom of his skis at the mid-sections will contact the snow while the tips and tails

---

[5] Speed further modifies the pole plant. For short turns at slow speeds, the pole is planted closer to the boot. For fast turns, the pole is planted farther down the hill.

protrude in the air. Under this condition a light circular motion of the body will easily turn the skis since resistance on the snow will be reduced markedly.

If the skier is in a hollow area (concave terrain), his skis will contact the snow at the tips and tails while the mid-sections are suspended in the air. Under this condition turning will be difficult, if not impossible.

These examples may be used as a guide to understand the principles of how terrain works for or against a skier seeking the most advantageous conditions to practice first parallel turns.

When the surface is hard-packed or icy, the skis meet little resistance in turning. In fact, a main concern is to keep the skis from "over-turning." However, as the snow becomes softer, wetter, and deeper, the turning process becomes increasingly difficult since the skis must displace heavier and larger amounts of snow.

It appears, from an empirical standpoint, that speed helps to turn the skis. However, the authors have consulted with several physicists and mechanical engineers, and have not received answers which are in agreement. It is suggested that in-depth research be conducted to find a scientific answer to this question.

HOP CHRISTIE

In the hop christie, the skis are held parallel and together throughout the turn; however, they leave the snow momentarily to change edges in the air. (See Fig. 7.2.)

Figure 7.2

Although the skier may hold the skis parallel and close together throughout the turn, he may experience difficulty in changing the edges quickly. The skier hops into the air in order to gain more time to change the edges. Thus, he is ready to land on a new set of edges prepared to contact the snow.

Hopping and displacing may be performed by lifting the tails, the tips, or the whole ski. Lifting the tails is the simplest and most frequently used form of initiation, although in softer snows this maneuver may result in driving the tips too deeply under the surface. Lifting the whole ski works better in wet and heavy snows. Lifting the tips (rearing) for a hop christie lies in the domain of a highly advanced maneuver.

Merely lifting the skis and dropping them back without changing the edges will result only in a vertical displacement without a change in direction. A change of direction requires an action up and to the side. A rotary movement of the whole body, after a rebounding force from the edges, is one method used to move in the direction of the turn, i.e., up, forward, around, and toward the inside of the turn. The skis will then follow the trunk alignment after a slight delay.

Retraction (As the trunk is lifted (up-unweighting) the legs are folded slightly under the pelvis. Another form of retraction occurs during the down unweighting at which time the tails are lifted *upward*. This form of movement is known as a "Ruade".) and displacement to the side with the angulated position is the second-most-used method for a hop christie. Note: Whether rotation or retraction-displacement is used to produce the hop, it will be considerably amplified by using one or both ski poles. Leaning forward and planting both poles for the initiation of each hop is suggested as an easy method for performing a series of short hops in a fall line, or for starting christies with shorter turning radii. These forms of initiation of a turn are useful on a steep slope. They also correct the habit of stemming, since the take-off requires the weight to be evenly distributed on both skis. They also provide a rapid angular displacement of the tails and more time to change the edges.

The hop christie's limitations are most marked in soft snow, where it becomes difficult to obtain proper support on the edges at initiation, and on ice, where excessive skidding occurs upon landing.

Another simplified method of executing a parallel turn is to start the turn by rolling only the edge of the outside ski into a new position while the inside ski is lifted slightly, and touches the snow only in the vicinity of the tip. To start a turn in this fashion, it is advisable to hold the skis wider apart during the initiation of the turn so that a comfortable weight shift might be obtained in pushing off with the lower *inside* ski to the upper *outside* ski. This movement resembles pedalling a bicycle where the legs move up and down, but never apart, as in stemming. This method of turning works well on packed slopes. In deep snows, however, the lack of weight on the inside ski may easily cause it to surface, hook, and spin the skier into a fall.

EXECUTION OF PURE PARALLEL CHRISTIES

Christie with Rotation

This is a parallel christie through turning the whole body in the direction of the turn.

Preparation. (Actions to Keep in Mind)

Bring the ski tips even.

Distribute the weight evenly on both skis.

Direct the tip of the lower pole forward, ready to be planted in the vicinity of the lower ski tip.

Lower the body position by bending the ankles, knees, and hip joints.

Initiation. (Actions to Keep in Mind)

Plant the pole.

Execute a springing movement of both skis upward, forward, around, and slightly toward the inside of the turn.

Release the edges at the moment of starting the turning impulse.

Steering. (Actions to keep in mind)

Bank for re-edging.

Lower the position dynamically, depending upon the radius of the turn.

Finishing.

Increase edging, and return to a traverse or stop.

Christie with Counter Rotation

This particular parallel christie derives its turning force from the legs pivoted in the direction of the turn.

Preparation. (Actions to Keep in Mind)

From a traverse, lower the body by bending the ankles, knees, and hip joints.

Increase weighting of the lower ski.

Prepare to plant the pole farther downhill slightly ahead of the lower binding.

Initiation. (Actions to Keep in Mind)

Use a "springy" upward movement in leg joints by obtaining the push predominantly from the lower leg.

Aid balance through pole support.

Turn the legs in the direction of the turn, and initiate side slipping.

Steering. (Actions to Keep in Mind)

Lower the body position.

Increase edging. (Angulation)

Apply progressive weighting on the outside ski of the turn.

Finishing. (Actions to Keep in Mind)

Increase pressure on the uphill edges.

Stop, or return to a new traverse position.

PARALLEL CHRISTIE WITH A CHECK

This maneuver is composed of two parallel turns. The first turn is executed into the hill, followed *immediately* by a turn across the fall line. The objective of this action is to *regulate the speed of descent,* and to *provide freedom in the selection of a starting place for the initiation of the turn to follow.* The *check* is also referred to as a *pre-turn* or *counter turn.*

The execution of first parallel turns becomes easier if the skier selects an angle of the traverse close to the fall line so that the speed will help him to be carried around, and the displacement of the skis will be easier. Caution: This may result in linking the turns with increasing speed to the point that the skier may lose control. Also, the selection of favorable terrain to start the turn is limited by the partially pre-determined curve of the christie.

At this point it becomes evident that a new skill is needed to maintain uniform speed and to control the path of descent.

In most skiing techniques the turning force of the *check* is derived mainly from the legs.[6] Example: The skier starts a short[7] christie uphill in which the tails are accelerated by the momentum of the sinking body. The skid is stopped rapidly by equally increased edging and weighting of both skis brought about by a *dynamic punch of both knees* upslope. In softer snow this movement builds up a platform of snow under the skis which helps to make the following turning and straightening actions more vigorous, comfortable, and efficient. It also places the skier in a low, stable, and aggressive position from which he starts the *re-coiling* (re-bounding) actions.

The momentum of the skier (forward and downhill) in a *check* is rapidly arrested, mainly at the level of his legs and skis. The trunk, however, tends to continue in the same direction. An analogy of this may be found in an automobile stopping suddenly, with the driver, as a consequence, leaning toward the steering wheel. The *role of the pole* at this point is very significant for it should be in a position *to permit it to absorb the remaining momentum of the trunk*.

Sequence of Execution

1. Select the spot to terminate a previous turn or traverse.
2. Execute the check and plant the pole.
3. Start the re-coiling action and the new turn in the new direction.

The check, as such, is a dynamic christie into the hill, and is a preparatory phase for a following turn. *It should not be considered in isolation, for the most difficult part is starting the next turn.*

An excellent approach to learning this useful maneuver is to practice "stop christies" from the fall line. In the stop christie the skier concentrates only on setting the edges and arresting the momentum of the trunk to "stop on a dime". Although the displacement of the skis in a stop christie is greater than in a check, the skier has to concentrate only on stopping and not on the turn which follows, which is often greater than $180°$.

---

[6] In this case the trunk is not a muscular turning force, but is relatively stable. It does not travel in the direction of the turn as fast as the legs; consequently, the trunk is delayed in a relative reverse position—also referred to as opposition.

[7] Standard displacement of the tails downhill varies approximately from a few inches to two feet.

For additional information, see Figure 7.3, phases in a parallel turn; 7.4, a check and follow-through with a split rotation; and 7.5, pole placement.

ERRORS AT THE PARALLEL LEVELS

Errors at the parallel level are numerous and often quite complex. Their underlying causes are frequently well hidden. The following remarks can be applied to most problems for which the skier seeks to find solutions and remedies.

Figure 7.3

Self Analysis

Analyze the problem by starting with the ski edges, and progressing to the upper parts of the body.

Read about the maneuver in technical ski literature, and compare it with your analysis.

Observe and analyze your ski tracks on the snow.

Try the maneuver in deeper and softer snow. This usually unearths well-hidden errors.

Observe your shadow on the snow if the sun is in a proper angle to project a clear silhouette.

Analysis Through Observation and Motion Pictures

Select a challenging terrain, and place three persons in positions which will enable them to observe you from the front, side, and back.

Figure 7.4

Figure 7.5

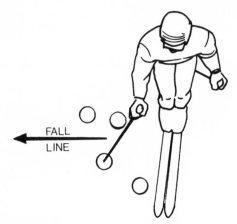

FALL LINE

Front Observer. Can best perceive *facial expressions* (may indicate fear of the fall line), *errors in angulation,* and the *pole plant.*

Side Observer. Can best perceive *lead change, sitting back or leaning forward,* and *hand movements relative to the trunk.*

Back Observer. Can best perceive *errors in timing, weight distribution,* and *edging.*

A good ski instructor, observing a skier for several runs, may detect various sources of trouble.

Motion Picture Camera or Video Tape. Arrange to have pictures taken from the front, side, and back and in slow motion, if possible. Analyze one movement at a time, e.g., pole plant, lead change, etc.

Your main goal is to obtain a correct "mental picture" of what you are trying to do. There is increasing evidence that "just thinking" about the performance of a skill and its analysis will bring improvement in the actual physical performance of it.

When possible, practice the skill while standing still. There is evidence that more complex ski movements may be divided into parts and practiced in stationary positions. For example, flexing movements and a pole plant, both a part of a parallel turn, may be practiced in a still position.

When the maneuver is mastered from a still position, practice the same action with the eyes closed. Next, practice on easy terrain under good snow conditions, and at slow speeds. Gradually increase the difficulty, but only if the previous steps have been well mastered.

ERRORS AND CORRECTIONS

Hop Christie

Error. Applying the turning force too late or too early when unweighting is not acting on the ski.

Correction. Synchronize unweighting with the turning force from a stationary position. Utilize a small hop with an accompanying displacement of the tails to the side.

Error. Inability to hop both skis simultaneously (Tendency to stem instead).

Correction. While traversing at slow speeds, lift the tails of both skis a few inches. Also practice hopping the entire surface of both skis a few inches uphill, and then a few inches downhill. Hop, and change slightly the direction of both skis.

Error. Difficulty or inability to change the edges during the hop, resulting in a "no turn maneuver".

Correction. Stand on a flat surface with the skis parallel, and lean forward while supported on the poles. With a small hop, lift and displace the tails to the side and land on the flat with the skis slightly edged. Repeat this exercise in the opposite direction.

Error. Improper use of the pole for support, and as an aid in balancing and timing.

Correction. Practice flexion and a simultaneous pole plant, placing it depending upon the turn. Practice the pole plant from a stationary position, and then in a slow fall line run. While displacing the skis only slightly, be aware that the pole is helping your straightening movements.

Error. Difficulty in initiating the skid due to the effect of landing on skis edged too sharply.

Correction. Repeat most of the forms of side slipping. Side slip between moguls, and change the edges and direction of the side slip at the tops of the moguls.

Pure Parallel Christies

Error. Hopping at the initiation of the turn.

Correction. Try starting the christies from a high position, and use down unweighting.

Error. "Over-turning" with the upper body, thus causing a "lost edge" and turning too far uphill at the finishing phase.

Correction. Place the outside hand of the turn at the base of the spinal column before initiating the turn. Hold the hand at the spinal column throughout the steering phase of the turn.

Error. Artificially reversed shoulders during the steering and finishing phase of the turn, resulting in a position without a purpose. (This often causes a fall due to unbalanced weight on the uphill ski.)

Correction. Keep both hands well in front of the hips. Angulate by lowering the outside shoulder, not by reversing it.

Error. Lifting the inside ski at the turn due to the habit of making turns by weight transfer.

Correction. Use a very small hop for initiation, and stress a simultaneous take-off from both skis.

Error. Lifting the inside ski at the turn due to an inability to turn and edge that ski.

Correction. Practice turns on the inside ski of the turn. Practice lifting the downhill ski in *traverses, uphill christies, christies from the fall line,* and finally, *when crossing the fall line.* Keep the outside ski one to two inches in the air, ready to return to a customary position when required for balance.

Special Turns

Special turns are generally parallel turns which demand adjustments that are dictated by unique *terrain* and *snow conditions.*

Individuality and freedom of movement in the execution of these turns are quite evident, since satisfactory results can be obtained through different means.

SHORT CHRISTIANIAS

These are successive short-radius christies close to the fall line in which the traverses are omitted, and the steering phase is shortened. These turns are also referred to as "Wedeln," "Godille," and "Short Swing." The techniques vary with the objectives. For example, maintaining a steady speed requires strong edging, while joyful swinging or acceleration of speed require a flatter position of the edges.

Short Christianias on Flat Skis

This is not a speed-regulating maneuver. In fact, it may be referred to as an accelerating swing, since the skier often increases his speed of descent with each turn.

The terrain for this maneuver should be shallow enough that the skier would not be afraid to schuss it. The skis usually turn very little from the fall line, and are kept rather flat. The term "flat" refers to the position of the edges, meaning that they are held *flatter*. In short, laborious weighting and edging are omitted, thus permitting the skier to retain an upright relaxed stance. The pole serves as a *timing device* rather than a support. Equally weighted skis, and turning force triggered *largely* by the legs (although possible by rotation), further characterize this stylish and enjoyable descent.

Short Christianias With Strong Edging (Linked Checks)

This is a practical type of turn on slopes with moguls and narrow passages that afford full control during the speed of descent. (See Fig. 8.1.) The maneuvers are characterized by:

Constant purposeful motion of the body parts.
Vigorously steered and edged skis across the fall line in a series of short radii.
Arrival at an angulated position.
A dynamic short steering phase of the turn, blending into initiation at the following turn.
Reliance of support on the pole.

Sequence of Performance

1. From a traverse, lower the body position by flexing the leg joints, and start a side slip.
2. Simultaneously, prepare the lower arm to plant the pole with the trunk facing the fall line.

Initiation

1. Plant the pole, followed by an energetic spring from both edges to unweight the skis and change the angle of the edges.
2. Initiate a side slip propelled by the turning force.

Steering

1. Execute a short steering phase combined with a sinking motion.
2. Continue the turning force, and terminate the skid by strong edging.

Figure 8.1

The above concise description does not tell the skier precisely "how to do it." Rather, it permits him to use his imagination in selecting movement patterns. The description which follows is *one* of many possible variations. (See Figs. 8.1 and 8.2.)

Figure 8.2

As a starting point, assume that the previous turn has been completed, and the skis are as equally weighted and edged as possible. The upper body and the legs are compressed, ready to recoil. The pole[8] is planted in line with the boots, thus reducing the remaining downhill momentum *of the trunk.*

The recoil is from both legs and the pole. The legs press from the uphill edges and project the body upward, forward, and toward the inside of the turn. Note: This movement should diminish the pressure on the skis, but should not lift them into the air.

During the light phase, the outside (upper) thigh directs the knee toward the inside of the turn, and with the ankle, helps to roll the edge.

As the outside ski makes firm contact with the snow, the adductor muscles of the thighs, which when contracted permit the legs to be held tightly together, must be relaxed to permit the inside ski to move forward about 2″ ahead of the outside ski. The legs are then pressed together again for the "new traverse." The outside leg continues turning and bending, and conveys the "drive" to the less active and less tense inside leg, which then starts to establish firm contact of the outside edge.

When both skis are in the vicinity of the fall line, they are firmly edged, and the pole is pulled out of the snow. The bending of the legs and trunk continues, resulting in a sinking motion of the body. The tails of the skis overtake the hips and shoulders as a result of the thighs turning faster than the trunk. The upper body leans toward the outside of the turn *in order to keep the body mass over the edges.*

The tip of the outside pole is directed forward, mainly from the wrist without a pronounced extension of the elbow or twisting of the spinal column. The edges are set, due to the increased tension of the ankle joints and to a final upslope thrust from the thighs and knees.

In another variation, split rotation may be used as a turning force. The skis may be pivoted near the tips (heel thrust) under the feet (swivel), or near the tails (tip thrust). The initiation may be a hop, unless the terrain is such that it lends itself to turning and unweighting. The skis may be held apart or together.

When skiing moguls, the terrain may be used in three degrees of difficulty.

1. Start the turn on top of the mogul, and edge for braking as you slide off the top. "Plunge"

[8] During standard short turns, when the pole acts as a support, it absorbs one-fourth to one-third of the skier's weight.

2. Ski in the groove between the moguls. "River Running"
3. Start the turn in the groove, and press the skis up the mogul. "Sideslip Uphill"

Adjustment to Powder Snow

Small amounts of powder snow, 12" to 18", require little physical adjustment, but may cause psychological problems since the skis are often submerged, and the skier cannot see the position of the tips. When the snow depth is 2' to 3', or is more compacted, the skier starts "floating." Adaptations, as follow, may be helpful.

Keep both skis equally weighted.

Ski close to the fall line.

Increase the turning force by projecting the hips in the direction of the turn, rotating the whole body, or making a hand movement in the direction of the turn.

Diminish the forward lean in the steering phase; instead, crouch.

Bend the knees and hips to the point where stability is increased without the loss of flexibility and quick reactions.

Clearly picture the bottoms of the skis *as a platform* on the snow, *not* as edging.

Amplify the "up-down" movements for easier changing of the "platform" surface of the skis.

Use thin, flexible skis that will slice the snow; and keep the tips on the surface.

Place the bindings one-half to one inch in back of standard binding locations.

Wax the skis so that the grooves on the bottoms are filled.

Drive the tips upward by pulling the toes and instep up while pressing on the heels.

When the surface of powder snow becomes cut up and partially packed by frequent tracks of skiers, it is advisable to increase the pressure on the tips during the steering phase in order to prevent the tips from bouncing on the uneven surface.

It is possible to turn in powder by submerging the whole ski length. Although this produces a well controlled curve of the turn, it is dangerous since the slopes may be littered with hidden branches or obstacles that can trap the tips. The following steps will permit the skier to become accustomed gradually to powder skiing:

1. Initiate the turn on packed snow, and enter the powder in the steering phase.
2. Perform a whole turn in the powder by starting from the fall line.
3. Perform one large radius turn at higher speeds to a stop.
4. To link turns, select a slope which will permit turning without requiring much braking.

Adjustments to Heavy, Soft, or Crusty Snow

In these conditions, the resistance to turning may increase to the point where initiation of a turn across the fall line becomes very difficult. If in addition, the surface is partially frozen, or has become wind-packed in random areas; thus alternately supporting and breaking under the skier's weight.

When snow heaviness or unpredictability make it dangerous to turn downhill, the skier should descend in a traverse, stop with a turn into the hill, execute a kick-turn (or step around), and so continue zig-zagging down the slope. Often, however, depending upon the strength, skill, balance, and experience of the skier, it is possible to displace the snow as follows:

1. Start with a check.
2. Plant the pole and feel the consistency of the snow as the pole penetrates.
3. Spring upward, lifting the skis evenly above the snow. (If needed, prolong the airborne position by quickly pulling the thighs toward the trunk.)
4. While in the air, change the leading ski, and turn both skis toward the fall line.
5. Upon landing, lower the outside ski to adapt to the incline for a simultaneous contact of both skis on the snow.
6. As the skis break through the crust, exert your strongest turning force.
7. Continue the turning force during the steering phase. Note: The skis often stop turning at the fall line if the skier fails to exert a continued propelling force.

Although the outside ski will do the "trail blazing" for the inside ski, the inside ski must be sufficiently weighted to slide in a similar plane, and not "pop" to the surface.

Through frequent skiing on difficult snows, the skier will develop a "snow sense" and turning power which will enable him to perform turns in heavy snows without hopping.

Adjustments to Ice

At times the slope freezes and becomes hard and icy. Places where frozen surfaces have been further compacted and smoothed out by a constant series of christies are referred to as "boiler plate." The equipment needed for skiing on icy slopes is: *quality slalom-type skis, with sharp edges,* and *good boots.* Also required are *strong legs,* and *no psychological restrictions.*

Major difficulties in skiing on ice lie in starting the turn, and preventing over-steering. Skiers who are used to performing christies with a check will at first feel uncomfortable on ice due to the lack of support from the edges at the moment of initiation. They must observe the following rules in order to learn edging instead of skidding:

Edges must retain continuous contact with the surface.

At the moment of initiation, *roll* the edges to the new position.

Diminish the up-down movement and unweighting.

Increase angulation for a better edge grip.

Balance the weight so that the entire length of the skis has an even pressure.

Shift all the weight to the outside ski where increased pressure at the edge is needed.

Hold the skis apart in order to gain support from the upper ski in places where the edges will not hold at all.

Start the turns with down-unweighting, and increase the pressure on the edge with a rising movement.

There are as many ways to perform turns in different types of snow as there are experts to describe them. Thus, there is no more technically perfect description of how to do it than: "If you wish to learn how to swim, you must get wet."

For further information on types of snow, refer to Figure 8.3, skiing in light powder; 8.4, skiing on ice; and 8.5, skiing in heavy spring snow.

ERRORS AND CORRECTIONS

Short Turns

Error. Taking too much time for the edge change, resulting in a wide-radius turn.

Correction. Usually taking too much time for the edge change is due to projecting the hips in the direction of the turn, resulting in tracking with a poor edge, and losing time in the process. One remedy is to use thigh (knee) displacement for the edge change. This process may take a long time to master but is well worth the effort. Another difficulty is starting the skis turning due to weak muscles. The following exercises will help: Practice dry land rotary turning motions; turn on top of the moguls; perform very slow turns on flat slopes.

Figure 8.3

Figure 8.4

Figure 8.5

Error. Using the pole plant *only* as a support or a timing device, resulting in heavy leaning into the hill, or a weak edge set.

Correction. Practice correct pole placement in a stationary position, eyes closed. In traverses hop from the lower pole. Execute stop christies and stress placing the weight on the downhill pole.

Powder Snow

Error. Waiting too long to start the next turn, resulting in a speed increase, and a consequent fear of entering the fall line.

Correction. Execute several downhill runs in a fall line. Practice christies to a stop. Pace yourself verbally, e.g., "pole plant and---now."

Error. Exaggerated continuous "back sitting," resulting in too much weight on the tails, which prevents them from swiveling.

Correction. Lower your position, and keep it balanced. Bend the knees and hips. Bend the trunk forward, and hold both hands in front. "Feel" your weight on the heels during the steering phase, with even weight on both feet at the initiation.

Error. Skiing powder in a too-erect position, resulting in a frequent loss of balance both forward and backward.

Correction. Ski with knees bent.

Icy Conditions

Error. Excessive unweighting or weighting, resulting in loss of contact with the snow, and slipping or overpowering the edge grip.

Correction. Weight the entire ski length as evenly as possible. Laborious weighting of the skis often overpowers the delicate edge grip, particularly when the skis are well across the fall line.

Error. Application of excessive turning force.

Correction. In order to avoid skidding and displacing the skis, use appropriate weighting, and take advantage of the skis carving capability.

Crud

Error. Indecision and fear of starting to turn downhill, resulting in skiing too far from the fall line.

Correction. A helpful exercise is to deliberately attack the slope with a series of jumps in the fall line, using support of both poles.

Error. Landing from a jump with too much weight on the inside ski.

Correction. Increase the angulated position upon landing. Lower the outside ski when airborne, and contact the snow with skis equally weighted.

Error. Trying to maintain classic, stylish positions and turning forces, which were learned on polished, packed, and manicured slopes.

Correction. ?

Fundamentals
of
Racing

CHAPTER

9

This chapter is meant for those who have mastered the minimum skiing skills, and are ready to advance to racing. The standard pupil progression offered by most ski schools is generally as follows: Beginners' classes progress from A (Beginners) to F (Short Swings). After E or F classes are completed, either special turns or beginning racing is offered.

Starting to race too early may divert the skier's effort from *skiing well* to *skiing fast*. Although an early exposure to racing may produce some good habits, it can also develop and magnify errors, and limit proper technique. Before entering the realm of racing, the skier should have mastered parallel turns and short swings. In addition, the racer needs the stamina to ski difficult mogul terrain without letting up, and the courage to enter turns at high speeds. On a race course, the skier has little time to decide when to start a turn, and little choice about where to turn.

It is critical that a skier's attitude towards turning change from a preoccupation with safety, stability, braking, and sideslipping, to risk, recovery, acceleration, and carving.

Downhill, slalom, and giant slalom are called alpine events. Giant slalom and slalom are usually the introductory events for a beginning racer. In order to

95

execute these events well, the skier must begin adding a number of efficient and sophisticated turns which are useful in the "fight against the stop watch."

SELECTED TECHNIQUES

Jet Turns

Jet turns are accelerated turns. The acceleration comes from projecting the body forward. The arms, upper body, hips, or legs may be projected in the direction of the turn to obtain relative acceleration of the skis.

There are numerous ways to jet (launch) a turn. However, no specific description will be attempted, since the resultant acceleration is the major item of significance. One often-used form of "jetting" is to push and turn the feet ahead of the body, directing the straightening movement backward, and at this moment achieving a relative acceleration of the skis. The skeletal system, for a moment, relies heavily on muscular strength to retain this position and return the trunk to a less strained form of balance.

The Serpent Turn

An analysis of techniques used by outstanding racers resulted in the designation of this turn. It presents an interesting concept of turning the skis with a minimum edge set and sideslip. Mastery of the turn demands long hours of practice, for the turning force lies in returning the alignment of the lower body with the anticipatory position of the trunk through relaxation, not contraction, of the muscles of the trunk. The analyzer was George Joubert, ski writer and technician, and Ski School Director at the University of Grenoble. The Grenoble University Ski Club administers a top racing team and a ski training program for 5800 students. Anticipation is a term used by the French or French-oriented ski schools. It denotes movements leading to positions directed downhill, which help in the execution of the oncoming turn. The movement may range from as little as an eye glance, selecting the terrain for the turn, to a gross body position such as the shoulders and chest facing and flexing downhill before the actual rotary action takes place. The "feel" of the turn is the key idea to keep in mind; a too-exhaustive description may lead to "paralysis by analysis."

In search for the "feel" of a serpent turn, observe these procedures:

1. Stay erect on the top of a bump, and place the downhill pole 1′ to 1½′ away from the ski and slightly behind the boot. Hold both hands in your line of vision with shoulders and chest twisted downhill.

2. Permit your trunk, through relaxation of back muscles, to tip 45° between the planted pole and the skis. A split second later, bend the knees to about a 90° angle. At this point the skis should start to turn, and the pressure should be felt on the tip of the outside ski.

3. In the steering (or guiding) phase, decrease the pressure on the tip, and straighten the body in the hollow of the mogul.

Using the above sequence to introduce yourself to the serpent turn, *avoid* the following:

1. Rotation of the hands and trunk.
2. Pronounced ankle bend.
3. Exaggerated downhill plunge of the trunk.
4. Knee flexion exceeding 90°.

The Skating Step

The mechanics of this action duplicate the dynamic movements of a speed skater, and, in some aspects, the more static herringbone climb. The object is to overcome the force of friction acting upon the skis through muscular effort. It is used most often on shallow or flat slopes where speed generally falls off. When on a traverse, the uphill ski is directed uphill and accelerated by a push from both the downhill ski and ski pole, and by a forward weight projection to the climbing ski. A gain in elevation will occur from this action, and is often needed to approach a gate in a slalom run.

An excellent exercise for developing power in skating steps, is to skate up a gentle hill, and strive for the longest possible glides through thrusting actions from alternate skis.

Cramponnage

This refers to retaining the line of the traverse on the uphill edge of the uphill ski, permitting in the meantime, the lower ski to be placed downhill, and at the desired angle.

Dodging and Speed-Regulating Positions

These positions have little effect upon the direction of the skis, but permit an increase or decrease in speed, and the evasion of the gate poles. Some examples:

1. For reducing speed, hold the body erect with the arms and hands extended sideward.
2. Factors that will help to increase speed are a minimal frontal exposure to air resistance, and an aerodynamic "egg shaped" stance.
3. Many positions permit the skis to pass very close to the gates without hooking the upper body: dodging with the hands or trunk, reversing the shoulders, and narrowing the frontal silhouette are most often used.

Bumpy Terrain

Overcoming bumpy terrain depends upon speed, snow conditions, contours and frequency of the bumps, radii and nature of the turns. Momentum on an upward profile of a mogul projects the skier into the air. Thus in one sense the mogul helps to unweight the skier; but if additional force is directed upward through the skier's quick rising, it will result in a jump or excessive unweighting.

Often a jump is the best way to go over chopped moguls. In this case speed, terrain, and muscular force must be coordinated to achieve the best takeoff, flight, and landing. When the skier is airborne, he can do little to change his trajectory other than to guess its length and prepare for a landing.

Actions which annul the upward projection of the skier at the top of a mogul and enable the skis to maintain contact with the snow, need to be appropriately timed. Some of these actions are *weight shifts, absorption,* and *flexing of the body parts.*

Shifting to a forward lean is good for retaining contact with the snow on bumps at slow speeds. The weight is centered over the balls of the feet, forcing the front of the skis to tip at the top of the mogul toward the downhill side. The action is similar to that of a teeter totter where the center of gravity shifts from one side to the other of the fulcrum.

A quick flexion (bending) of the body produces instant unweighting, followed by weighting and a lowering of the center of gravity. The force of the weighting conveyed to the skis compresses the snow, and causes the skis to "cling" to the mogul contours. The timing of this action is critical.

Avalement

This technique of absorption means literally to swallow (the bumps). It is a form of absorption of the moguls where, as a result of a shortening of the abdominal muscles, and the muscles connecting the thighs and pelvis, the trunk and thighs are pulled toward each other. This movement takes place as the skis ascend the mogul. The degree of flexion is greatest at the top of the mogul. This produces a shock absorbing effect and, when executed quickly, a form of down-unweighting. From the top of the mogul the straightening movement begins to aid the skis to retain contact with the snow. The return to a more extended position provides the stance from which the cycle may be repeated.

Common errors in the execution of an avalement are:

A "back sitting" position without the straightening phase.

Lowering and flexing the trunk resulting in compaction of the body rather than the desired shock-absorbing effect.

Carving

Here, basic ski-turning characteristics, (i.e., side cut and flexibility of the skis) are combined with purposeful weight shifts and positions in order to produce a carving track with a minimum of sideslipping. The body joints nearest the skis exert a delicate edge control. Lateral stiffness of the boots is also important, although too-tightly-locked boots may impede the ankle joint, and diminish the "edgesense" of the feet.

Slalom skis have the greatest built-in turning characteristics, while downhill skis have the least. Relying *only* on the side cut characteristics of the skis will produce a turn with a very large radius. To tighten up a turn, the flexibility of the skis must be taken advantage of, since a flexible ski will become concave under the combination of the skier's weight and centrifugal force, and thus serve to shorten the radius of the turn.

Edging and bending the outside ski of the turn while also lifting the tail of the inside ski is a good way to begin learning carving, since the skier may concentrate fully on weight distribution and edge angle for *only one ski*. Carving of *both skis* held slightly apart requires a detailed study of both fore and aft, and side to side balance.

Downhill (D.H.)

The opportunity for practicing downhill running for a recreational skier is limited due to crowded slopes and to difficulty in finding slopes of adequate gradient and surface. To practice long descents safely at high speeds, the skier must be sure that there will be few people on the slope so that he may concentrate on the required techniques without the apprehension of skiers crossing his line. Early mornings and last runs, just prior to the time that the ski patrol closes the trail, seem to be the best times.

The most frightening aspect of learning downhill running is the unaccustomed acceleration. The skier must remember that on any given slope, there is a point where the skis do not accelerate any more. This is generally called "terminal velocity." At this point speed may be quite enjoyable, since it is constant.

Longer and heavier skis with less side cut, softer tips, and stiffer tails are used for downhill. Championship courses are generally 2 mi. long, and are skied at speeds ranging from 50 to 75 miles per hour. The course has approximately 25 control gates which are 27′ wide. Downhill courses at the local level, and special women's courses, are generally less demanding.

Giant Slalom (G.S.)

The turns in a G.S. have medium radii, and the skier may enter traverses between the turns. Many experts consider the G.S. championships to be the most technical of all the events.

Simple G.S. courses for beginning racers resemble the typical descent of a recreational skier during free skiing.

A recommended prelude to the G.S. course is simply to practice non-stop runs, carving medium to long radius turns as one's ability permits. If a skier wants to mark the line of his descent, he should use nothing stiffer than small evergreen branches in order to diminish the danger to the other recreational skiers.

Although not in the same degree as downhill, the demands of space for G.S. turns will interfere with the general ski area operation. Championship G.S. courses for men last approximately 90 to 120 seconds, and cover at least 30 gates. The course drops at least 400 meters (1,312.333') for men, and 300 meters (9,843') for women. The gate width is usually 20'.

Slalom

The word *slalom* comes from the old Scandinavian "slalam" which means "interrupted course." A slalom course is defined by gates which are set at various angles to the fall line, and close to it. Although their order may vary, there are three kinds of slalom gates. They are called *open, closed*, and *oblique*. See Figure 9.1 which illustrates #1 as an open gate, #2 as a closed gate (sometimes referred to as a blind gate), and #3 as an oblique gate. (See Figure 9.1.) A slalom requires little space, and thus may be practiced, in simplified form, without interfering with the general ski area operation. Ski school and NASTAR races often offer simple slalom courses for recreational skiers. In this type of race recreational skiers compare their times with the "pace setter." Pace setters are usually among the best of the local area skiers.

When slalom poles are not available, one may practice controlled turns by:

1. Turning at imaginary gates and pre-determined spots in free skiing.
2. Skiing closely behind another skier, and following in the exact pattern of his track.
3. Turning around dye-marked spots or evergreen branches on the slope.
4. Skiing between trees. (A fun, but not a forgiving form of play.)

Should one wish to try the course of a local racing team, first request permission from the person in charge. The first time down, begin at the starting gate, or a little below it, and ski slowly just to "make it." It will be quite natural at this stage to be able to ski only

Figure 9.1

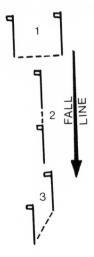

6 or 7 gates, and to experience frustration because of the seeming difficulty.

Courses set for racers are usually close to the fall line, and are deeply rutted. One approach to ski this type of course is to round the turns more widely, and ski outside of the ruts. If the course is not too difficult, and the skier decides to stick with it, he should offer assistance in setting the poles, packing the course through side slipping, and putting the poles away after his practice sessions.

If you decide to run gates alone, choose an appropriate place, e.g., at the edge of a trail. First, set a well-spaced single pole slalom. (See Fig. 9.2) Later, try well-spaced open gates, and eventually tighten the gates, using various gate combinations. In the early stages, *full control* should be the chief objective. Avoid errors in selecting a line of descent as shown in Figure 9.3, where only the dotted line shows the *correct* line of descent. After completing practice sessions, it is common courtesy to remove and bundle the poles, and smooth out the ruts in the snow.

Championship slalom for men requires each racer to make two runs through 55 to 75 gates. Women are required to make two runs through 40 to 60 gates. Each gate includes a pair of poles topped with flags colored blue, red, and yellow. The width of a slalom gate is a minimum of 10'. The vertical drop is from 180 meters (590′ 6″) to 220 meters (721′ 9″) for men, and from 120 meters (393′ 9″) to 180 meters for women.

Slalom is currently undergoing innovations such as racing through alternate sides of single poles in a single pole slalom, and setting two adjacent courses which permit two racers to compete side by side at the same time. Perhaps someday a cross gate requiring a jump will add a new dimension to this interesting event. (See Fig. 9.4)

Figure 9.2

Figure 9.3

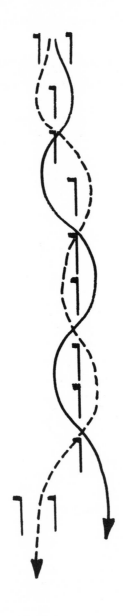

Figure 9.4

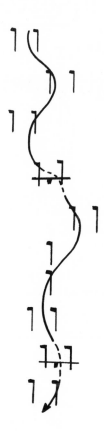

Etiquette and Equipment

ETIQUETTE

Rules and codes of conduct are necessary to help maintain safety on the slopes just as they are necessary in driving or boating. Conscientious adherance to them helps to decrease accidents significantly.

As in the application of most safety rules, alertness and common sense are of utmost importance. Some of the more basic forms of common courtesies to uphold are:

1. Observe traffic signs and posted areas. They have been prepared carefully for the safety of *all* skiers.

2. Ski under *control* which means having the ability to avoid stationary objects and skiers at all times.

3. If it is necessary to stop, check to see that it is not in an area which will obstruct or impair the passage of other skiers.

4. An overtaking skier is responsible for avoiding the skier below him.

5. When nearing an intersection of a trail, check for approaching skiers.

6. When overtaking another skier, pass to the right.

7. When starting, always check for approaching skiers.

8. Always wear safety straps to prevent losing a ski. Runaway skis are dangerous missiles.

9. If it is necessary to walk or climb in a ski area, be sure to wear skis or else move to the side of the trail or slope.

10. Await your turn at the lift.

11. While carrying skis in a congested area, use caution in turning around in order to avoid hitting surrounding skiers.

EQUIPMENT

Innovation and change are bywords of the 1970's. Ski attire and equipment are no exceptions to the era.

Scientific advances are being made so rapidly that attire and equipment which seemed quite modern a few years ago are now quite outdated.

For this reason, a beginning skier should rent equipment at first, perhaps until the third or fourth outing. It is strongly recommended, however, that he rent quality material, for without it he could easily miss the safety, comfort, and fun which good equipment helps to provide.

When ready to buy, check the current literature, particularly skiing magazines which have continuous articles on the important factors to consider on the latest equipment. In short, make careful comparisons.

Quality of boots is particularly important, since cheap or inferior ones break down easily and lose the necessary rigidity required for good skiing. Lace boots are rapidly being replaced by the buckle boot and the ratchet-type boot. Another recent innovation in boots is the "pour inner," designed to solve the fitting problem. There are basically two materials used to pour and form the inner boot. One is a liquid urethane elastomer that sets like rubber, and the other is an aerated urethane called foam. Both materials are quite new, and time is needed to evaluate them more precisely. It is well to keep in mind that the "pour inner" boots might not have good resale value since they are fitted for a specific individual, and replacement of the pour inner material is rather costly.

As for poles, there appears to be a trend toward shorter lengths, and about a fifty-fifty split in preference between aluminum and steel.

Metal, fiberglass, and reinforced fiberglass skis are more durable, and easier to use than wooden skis, but are also more expensive. In determining the appropriate length, one needs to consider his level of ability, and the type of terrain he will most often be skiing on. Shorter skis (approximately head height) are usually better for the beginner, while more advanced skiers would use longer skis.

Ski apparel is quite varied. Common sense indicates the importance of protective clothing that is warm, but which allows great freedom of movement. Elegance in attire, however, can be ego-bolstering and thus provide certain people with a sense of well-being. Again, it is suggested that the skiing magazines are the best sources of information on equipment and clothing; they not only provide current information, but also predict future trends.

Secondhand Equipment

Another method of obtaining equipment is through "ski swaps" which are conducted in most ski centers.

Many times good buys can be obtained by checking the bulletin boards at ski lodges. They often contain notices for the sale of ski equipment by private parties. Skis turned in by racers are often good buys for recreational skiers. Some ski shops allow tryouts of new models before purchase.

Refurbished Equipment

If ski poles are too long, they may be shortened. Skis may be modified by relocating the bindings, correcting the grooves, and by sharpening and repairing the edges. Used skis may be renewed by the manufacturer.

The "pour inner" material may be removed from the shell of a "pour inner" boot, and customed fitted again.

Suggested Readings

The Official American Ski Technique, The Professional Ski Instructors of America, Inc., 945 East First South, Salt Lake City, Utah 84102, 1966.

> This edition is a large format of 168 pages covering a history of skiing, ski mechanics, and biomechanics. It includes an outline analyzing and correcting errors in ski techniques. There is a special section on avalanches, and a detailed listing of teaching progressions.

The New Official Austrian Ski System. Translated by Ronald Palmedo. New York: A.S. Barnes and Company, 1961.

> A classic text on the Austrian technique, and includes excellent sequence photographs and drawings. There are also descriptions of terrain for executing various maneuvers. The text stresses counter-rotation as a turning force. There is a particular emphasis on the beginning stages of skiing.

Advisory Committee on the Teaching of the French Skiing Method, *Handbook for the Teaching of the French Skiing Method.* Translated by Betty Palmedo, Boissy and Colomb, Grenoble, France, 1967.

> A concise, but analytic, description of skiing maneuvers. It deals with many special turns in various snows, and suggests the use of rotation in the early stages of skiing. It deals with all forms of turning forces for more advanced skiers. There is a section on teaching children.

O'Conner, Loarne "Oakie." *The Canadian Ski Technique.* Toronto and Montreal: McClelland and Stewart Limited, 1965.

> Deals with the ski instruction techniques of the Canadian Ski Instructors Alliance There is a concise description of skiing maneuvers, common faults, and a selection of terrain for the best execution. The photographs and drawings are good. A final section includes racing techniques.

Joubert, Georges and Vuarnet, Jean. *How to Ski the New French Way.* Translated by Sim Thomas and John Fry. New York: The Dial Press, 1967.

> Converts useful elements of skiing maneuvers observed in international racing to recreational skiing. There are well-described sections on the serpent turn and avalement. Stress is placed on adaptation to difficult snows and terrain. It also includes chapters on racing techniques for slalom, giant slalom, and downhill.

McCulloch, Ernie. *Ski the Champion's Way.* New York: Harper and Row, Publishers, 1967.

> Has numerous photographs. It contains information from beginning skiing to elements of racing, and also includes jumps and trick skiing.

Lund, Morten. *The Skier's Bible.* New York: Doubleday and Company, 1968.

> Contains good general information, as well as 300 photographs. It includes a review of the American Ski Technique, "Nature Teknik," short ski technique, progressions, history, safety, etiquette, and where to ski in the United States and Canada.

Ski. Universal Publishing and Distributing Corporation, 235 East Fourth St., New York, New York, 10017.

> A magazine containing feature articles and profiles of ski personalities. It provides an excellent analysis of racing problems and events. In addition, it includes short articles on travel, ski fashions, and pointers on ski instruction.

Skiing. Ziff-Davis Publishing Company, One Park Avenue, New York, New York, 10016.

A magazine containing articles on equipment, instruction, travel, competition, and special features. There is an objective description of ski equipment and of innovations. It is currently featuring a series of articles on instruction and techniques supported by explicit drawings.

Ski Racing. Paper House Inc., 1801 York, Denver, Colorado, 80206.

This is a weekly newspaper (during the winter months) which lists the results of local, national, and international competition. It features articles on ski racing.

407063

GV
854
.T9

107069

GV
854   Twardokens, George
.T9   Skiing

107069

Learning Resources
Brevard Community College
Cocoa, Florida